DORDT INFORMATION SERVICES

3 6520 0041288 $

D0822315

Poor Women, Poor Families

Poor Women, Poor Families

Revised Edition

The Economic Plight of America's Female-Headed Households

Harrell R. Rodgers, Jr.

M. E. SHARPE, INC.
ARMONK, NEW YORK
LONDON, ENGLAND

Copyright © 1990 by M. E. Sharpe, Inc.

All rights reserved. No part of this book may be reproduced in any
form without written permission from the publisher, M. E. Sharpe, Inc.,
80 Business Park Drive, Armonk, New York 10504.

Available in the United Kingdom and Europe from M. E. Sharpe,
Publishers, 3 Henrietta Street, London WC2E 8LU.

Library of Congress Cataloging-in-Publication Data

Rodgers, Harrell R.
    Poor women, poor families: the economic plight of America's female-
headed households / by Harrell R. Rodgers, Jr. —revised ed.
    p. cm.
    Includes bibliographical references.
    ISBN 0-87332-594-X—ISBN 0-87332-595-8 (pbk.)
    1. Women heads of households—United States. 2. Poor women—
welfare—United States.   I. Title.
HV1445.R64   1990
362.83'0973—dc20   89-24372
                                                                  CIP

Printed in the United States of America

                        ∞

MV   10   9   8   7   6   5   4   3   2   1

Contents

Figures and Tables

Figures

Tables

Acknowledgments

In preparing this revised edition I have had the good fortune of having both excellent research assistants and a growing body of exemplary research to draw upon. David Flores, Marla Bird, Gabrielle Forrest, and Michael Speckhard played a very important role by copying articles and tracking down dozens of budgets and a few hundred obscure facts and figures. Marla also designed many of the tables. To each of them my warmest and sincerest thanks.

Fortunately, the volume and quality of research on poverty continues to grow. Any value this book may have is the direct result of the superb body of research that continues to be produced by a very dedicated and talented body of scholars.

Pat Kolb of M. E. Sharpe suggested this second edition and convinced me to see it through. Bessie Blum did an excellent job of copy editing the manuscript, and Michael Weber and Laura Schackman orchestrated the manuscript through press. To each I extend my heartiest gratitude.

My wife, Lynne, continues to be a source of strength and inspiration. I am more grateful than I can express for her partnership and love. Lannie and Lissie, though preteens, remind me that they are by now too mature and worldly for unsophisticated nicknames. So, to Elaine and Melissa, all my love.

Harrell Rodgers
Houston, Texas
November 1989

Poor
Women,
Poor
Families

Chapter 1

The Increase in Poor Households Headed by Women

By far the largest group of poor people in America is made up of single women and their children. Over half of all the poor people in America live in households headed by a woman. Female-headed households suffer a rate of poverty that is almost six times greater than the rate for married-couple families. Yet, female-headed families are the fastest growing household type in the nation. Between 1959 and 1987 the number of female-headed households with children almost tripled. Over half of all the children living in these households lived in poverty. The poverty rate for female-headed families is the primary reason why poverty among American children has increased dramatically over the last fifteen years. American children suffer a rate of poverty that exceeds 20 percent, and they are the poorest age group in America. Where poverty is concerned, it is a great deal safer to be old than young in America.

What is the cause of the economic deprivation that savages such a massive proportion of all members of female-headed households? The basic theme of this book is that the primary problem is the failure of American social programs to keep pace with immense and fundamental alterations in family demographics.

The United States—indeed, the entire Western industrial

world—is undergoing a major revolution. The revolution is obvious but often subtle in its complexity and impact. Some of its most manifest implications either have gone unnoticed, have been purposefully ignored, or have yet to be fully understood. The revolution is the change that is taking place in women's roles. The changes are major, and continuing. They portend extensive alterations in family structures, the economy, the political system, and society in general.

The Alteration in Women's Status and Roles

Throughout the twentieth century women have struggled, with considerable success, to alter their status and roles. In the first half of the century women organized to gain such basic rights as the franchise, the right to own property, and standing to sue in a court of law. Hard-won victories in these areas ended women's status as property (Chafe 1972; Freeman 1975; Murphy 1973; Ross 1973; Smith 1979).

In the second, and current, phase of the women's movement, the emphasis is on gaining legal and social equality. This phase has witnessed the large-scale entry of women into the job market (Bergman 1989; Fuchs 1989; Smith and Ward 1989). In 1960, women comprised 33 percent of the work force. By 1988, 45 percent of the total work force was female. In 1960, about 38 percent of all women were employed. By 1988, 56 percent were employed, bringing the female work force up to 54 million. Of all full-time employees working year-round, women constituted 39 percent in 1988. Almost 30 million women held full-time, year-round jobs.

Not only are more women in the work force, but the marital status of women presently working has also changed. In 1940, 64 percent of all employed women were single, widowed, or divorced. By 1988, single, divorced, and widowed women were even more likely to be in the work force, but married women had increased their participation rate to the extent that they comprised the vast

Table 1.1

Women's Participation in the Labor Force

Married with Children under Age 6		Married with Children under Age 1	
1950	11.9%	1976	31.0%
1955	16.2	1978	35.3
1960	18.6	1980	38.0
1965	23.3	1982	43.9
1970	30.3	1983	43.1
1975	36.6	1984	46.7
1980	41.5	1985	48.4
1985	53.4	1986	49.8
1987	56.8	1987	50.8

Source: Bureau of the Census 1987, *Statistical Abstract of the United States 1988* 108th ed. (Washington, D.C.: GPO), p. 374.

majority of all working women. Indeed, increased employment rates have been greatest for women with children. The largest proportional increase has been among women with children under the age of six. The figures in table 1.1 show how dramatically the labor participation rate of women with children has changed in recent years.

The impact of these changing roles cannot be exaggerated. Since 1980 there have been more families in the United States with both husband and wife working than families with only the husband working (Bureau of the Census 1983a, 413). Most women work out of sheer necessity. Some two-thirds of all working women are their families' sole supporters, provide for themselves, or have husbands who earn less than $15,000.

The changes in women's status and roles have been accompanied by another sign of greater freedom and independence: greatly increased rates of divorce, marital separation, and out-of-wedlock births. The result is that women in significantly increasing numbers are becoming the heads of American households. The Census Bureau distinguishes three types of female-headed households:

Table 1.2

Families with Children under 18 by Type, Selected Years, 1959–1987

	Total families (in 1000s)	Female-headed families (in 1000s)	Percent of total	Other families (in 1000s)	Percent of total
1987	33,957	7,151	21.0	26,806	78.9
1986	33,800	7,095	21.0	26,705	79.0
1985	33,535	6,892	20.5	26,643	79.5
1984	32,941	6,832	20.7	26,109	79.3
1983	32,723	6,609	20.2	26,114	79.8
1982	32,567	6,397	19.6	26,170	80.4
1981	32,587	6,488	19.9	26,099	80.1
1980	32,772	6,299	19.2	26,473	80.8
1978	31,735	5,837	18.4	25,898	81.6
1977	31,637	5,709	18.0	25,928	82.0
1976	31,430	5,310	16.9	26,120	83.1
1975	31,377	5,119	16.3	26,258	83.7
1974	31,331	4,922	15.7	26,409	84.3
1973	30,997	4,597	14.8	26,400	85.2
1972	30,810	4,322	14.0	26,488	86.0
1971	30,724	4,076	13.3	26,648	86.7
1970	30,071	3,837	12.8	26,243	87.2
1969	29,995	3,384	11.3	26,611	88.7
1968	29,323	3,269	11.1	26,054	88.9
1967	29,032	3,190	11.0	25,842	89.0
1963	28,317	2,833	10.0	25,484	90.0
1959	26,992	2,544	9.4	24,448	90.6

Source: Bureau of the Census (1988), "Money Income and Poverty Status of Families and Persons in the United States: 1987," *Current Population Reports*, series P-60, no. 161.

- *family household*: two or more related persons living together;
- *nonfamily household*: two or more unrelated persons of the same or opposite sex living together;
- *single household*: one adult living alone.

Since the late 1950s the proportion of all three types of households headed by a woman has increased by over 50 percent. By 1987, 16 percent of all households were headed by a woman: 13

Figure 1.1 **Percentage of Families Headed by a Female with Children, 1987**

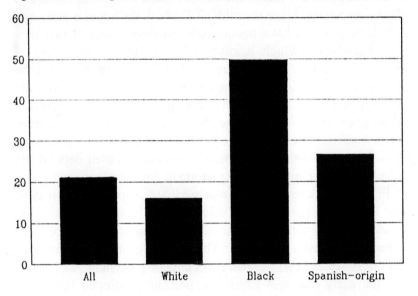

percent for whites, 23 percent for those of Spanish origin, and 43 percent for blacks.

Even more important, in 1959 only one in every eleven families with children was female-headed. Between 1959 and 1987 the number of female-headed families with children increased by 181 percent. The number of male-headed families increased by only 9.6 percent. In 1987 one of every five families with children under eighteen was headed by a woman (see table 1.2). This included 16 percent of all white families, 27 percent of all Spanish-origin families, and 50 percent of all black families (see figure 1.1).

The Feminization of Poverty

Despite the fact that the changes documented here are enormous, have persisted over at least two decades, and do not seem to be abating, public policies have not been altered to respond to these transformations. The consequences are reflected in part by the crisis that presently faces millions of female household heads and their dependents. Since the mid-1970s, both the popular press and scholarly journals have become increasingly aware of this new social problem, which is often labeled the "feminization of poverty" (Burlage 1978; Cooney 1979; Pearce 1978). The term refers to the growing percentage of all poor Americans who are women, and their dependents. Recent increases in the proportion of all poor living in female-headed families or households have been dramatic. The rising poverty rate among women has been so significant that over the last decade women and their dependents have become the major poverty group in America.

Figure 1.2 shows the huge increase that occurred between 1960 and 1987 in the percentage of all the poor who live in households headed by a woman. In 1960 about 27 percent of all the poor lived in female-headed households.* The percentage increased through-out the 1960s and early 1970s, exceeding 50 percent in 1976. During the early and mid-1980s the percentage dipped below 50 percent in some years but exceeded 50 percent again in 1986 and 1987. Despite the fact that women headed only 16 percent of all households and 21 percent of all families with children in 1987, *52 percent of all the poor lived in female-headed households.* The change has been substantial for poor whites but even greater for minorities. In 1987, 45 percent of poor whites, 43 percent of all poor of Spanish origin, and 71 percent of the black poor lived in female-headed households (see table 1.2, table 2.2, and figure 1.2).

As chapter 2 will detail, a critical feature in the feminization of poverty has been the enormous increase in the percentage of all households headed by women. As women head more households, poverty increases because female-headed households endure exceptionally high rates of poverty. In 1987, for example, only 6.0

---

* The quality of the Social Security Administration's data for the years 1959 to 1964 is somewhat suspect. These data were retrospective and some of the differences between late 1959 and the early 1960s may reflect problems with collection and reporting. For a more in-depth analysis of these problems, see Rodgers 1978, and Rodgers 1982, 14–27.

Table 1.3

Poverty Schedule: Family of Four (Nonfarm), 1959–1987

	Standard	Millions of poor	% of total pop.
1959	$2,973	39.5	22.0
1960	3,022	39.9	22.0
1961	3,054	39.9	22.0
1962	3,089	38.6	21.0
1963	3,128	36.4	19.0
1964	3,169	36.1	19.0
1965	3,223	33.2	17.0
1966*	3,317	30.4	16.0
1966	3,317	28.5	15.0
1967	3,410	27.8	14.0
1968	3,553	25.4	13.0
1969	3,743	24.1	12.0
1970	3,968	25.4	13.0
1971	4,137	24.1	11.0
1972	4,275	25.4	12.0
1973	4,540	23.0	11.5
1974*	5,038	24.3	12.0
1974	5,038	24.3	11.5
1975	5,500	25.9	12.0
1976	5,815	25.0	12.0
1977	6,200	24.7	12.0
1978	6,662	24.7	11.4
1979	7,412	26.1	11.7
1980	8,414	29.3	13.0
1981	9,287	31.8	14.0
1982	9,862	34.4	15.0
1983	10,178	35.3	15.2
1984	10,609	33.7	14.4
1985	10,989	33.1	14.0
1986	11,203	32.4	13.6
1987	11,600	32.5	13.5

Source: Bureau of the Census, "Money Income and Poverty Status of Families and Persons in the United States," *Current Population Reports,* series P-60, various years.
*Revision in census calculations.

Table 1.4

Poverty Rate for Families, by Type of Family, Race, and Spanish Origin, 1959–1987

	All families				Families with female householder, no husband present				All other families			
	All races	White	Black	Spanish-origin	All races	White	Black	Spanish-origin	All races	White	Black	Spanish-origin
1987	10.8	8.2	29.9	25.8	34.3	26.7	51.8	51.8	6.3	5.5	13.6	17.9
1986	10.9	8.6	28.0	24.7	34.6	28.2	50.1	51.2	6.3	5.7	12.1	16.5
1985	11.4	9.1	28.7	25.5	34.0	27.4	50.5	53.1	7.0	6.3	13.1	17.1
1984	11.6	9.1	30.9	25.2	34.5	27.1	51.7	53.4	7.2	6.4	14.7	16.7
1983	12.3	9.7	32.4	26.3	36.0	28.3	53.8	53.5	7.8	7.0	16.2	18.1
1982	12.2	9.6	33.0	27.2	36.3	27.9	56.2	55.4	7.9	7.0	16.4	18.9
1981	11.2	8.8	30.8	24.0	34.6	27.4	52.9	53.2	7.0	6.3	15.6	15.4
1980	10.3	8.0	28.9	23.2	32.7	25.7	49.4	51.3	6.3	5.6	14.3	15.4
1979	9.2	6.9	27.8	20.3	30.4	22.3	49.4	49.2	5.5	4.8	13.2	13.0
1978	9.1	6.9	27.5	20.4	31.4	23.5	50.6	53.1	5.3	4.7	11.8	12.4
1977	9.3	7.0	28.2	21.4	31.7	24.0	51.0	53.6	5.5	4.8	13.5	13.2
1976	9.4	7.1	27.9	23.1	33.0	25.2	52.2	53.1	5.6	4.9	13.5	15.6
1975*	9.7	7.7	27.1	25.1	32.5	25.9	50.1	53.6	6.2	5.5	14.2	17.6
1974	8.8	6.8	26.9	21.2	32.1	24.8	52.2	49.6	5.4	4.7	13.2	14.7

Year											
1974*	9.2	7.0	27.8	21.3	32.5	24.9	52.8	49.6	5.7	4.9	14.2	14.7
1973	8.8	6.6	28.1	19.8	32.2	24.5	52.7	51.4	5.5	4.6	15.4	13.1
1972	9.3	7.1	29.0	n.a.	32.7	24.3	53.3	n.a.	6.1	5.3	16.2	n.a.
1971	10.0	7.9	28.8	n.a.	33.9	26.5	53.5	n.a.	6.8	5.9	17.2	n.a.
1970	10.1	8.0	29.5	n.a.	32.5	25.0	54.3	n.a.	7.2	6.2	18.6	n.a.
1969	9.7	7.7	27.9	n.a.	32.7	25.7	53.3	n.a.	6.9	6.0	17.9	n.a.
1968	10.0	8.0	29.4	n.a.	32.3	25.2	53.2	n.a.	7.3	6.3	19.9	n.a.
1967	11.4	9.0	33.9	n.a.	33.3	25.9	56.3	n.a.	8.7	7.4	25.3	n.a.
1966	11.8	9.3	35.5	n.a.	33.1	25.7	59.2	n.a.	9.3	7.7	27.6	n.a.
1966*	12.7	10.2	n.a.	n.a.	35.1	27.8	n.a.	n.a.	10.0	8.4	n.a.	n.a.
1965	13.9	11.1	n.a.	n.a.	38.4	31.0	n.a.	n.a.	11.1	9.2	n.a.	n.a.
1964	15.0	12.2	n.a.	n.a.	36.4	29.0	n.a.	n.a.	12.5	10.5	n.a.	n.a.
1963	15.9	12.8	n.a.	n.a.	40.4	31.4	n.a.	n.a.	13.1	11.0	n.a.	n.a.
1962	17.2	13.9	n.a.	n.a.	42.9	33.9	n.a.	n.a.	14.3	12.0	n.a.	n.a.
1961	18.1	14.8	n.a.	n.a.	42.1	33.5	n.a.	n.a.	15.4	13.1	n.a.	n.a.
1960	18.1	14.9	n.a.	n.a.	42.4	34.0	n.a.	n.a.	15.4	13.0	n.a.	n.a.
1959	18.5	15.2	48.1	n.a.	42.6	34.8	65.4	n.a.	15.8	13.3	43.3	n.a.

Source: Bureau of the Census, ''Money Income and Poverty Status of Families and Persons in the United States,'' *Current Population Reports*, series P-60, various years.

Note: Persons of Spanish origin may be of any race.

*Based on revised methodology.

Figure 1.2 **Percentage of Poor in Female-headed Households**

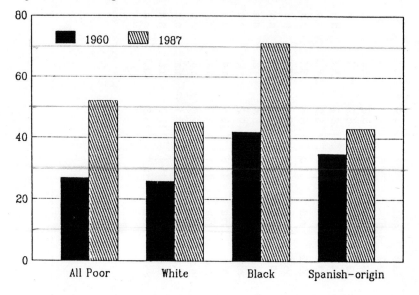

Figure 1.3 **Poverty Rate of Families by Type and Race, 1987**

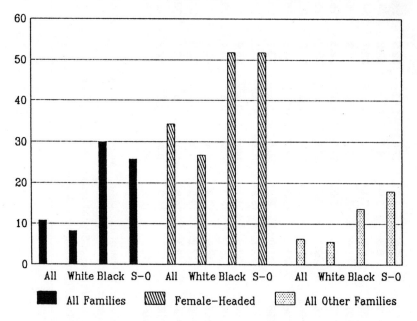

Figure 1.4 **Poverty Rate of Children**

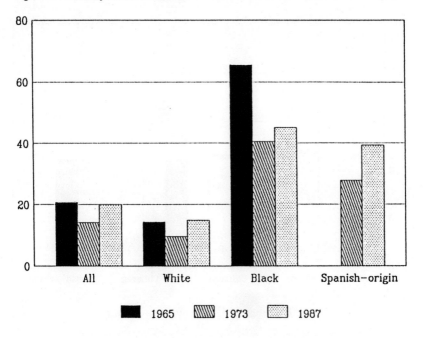

percent of all married couple families fell below the poverty line. The poverty rate for female-headed households was almost six times greater, at 34.3 percent. The rate for white female-headed households was very high (about 26.7 percent), but for black and Spanish-origin female-headed households, it was over 50 percent (see table 1.4 and figure 1.3).

Poverty among Children

One of the most ominous consequences of the high rates of poverty for women who head families is the deprivation brought to their dependent children. As more and more women have fallen below the poverty level, poverty rates among children have increased very significantly. Since 1982 poverty among children has averaged over 20 percent. This is the highest rate of poverty for children since

Figure 1.5 **Percentage of Poor Children in Female-headed Households**

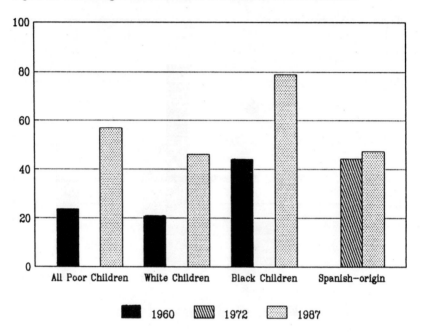

the early 1960s. As figure 1.4 shows, the rate of poverty was higher for children of all races in 1987 than in 1973. One in five children in America now lives in poverty. This includes 15 percent of all white children, 39 percent of all children of Spanish origin, and over 45 percent of all black children.

More than half of all the poor children in America now live in female-headed families, compared with 25 percent in the late 1950s and early 1960s (see figure 1.5). In 1987 there were 7.1 million poor children living in female-headed families; this represents a 71 percent increase since 1959. By the 1970s an average of 53 percent of all poor children in America lived in female-headed families, with a high of 58.5 percent in 1978. The average for 1980–1987 was 53.2 percent.

The poverty rate for children in female-headed families has remained over 50 percent in every year since 1959 save one (in

1979 it was 48.6 percent) (Bureau of the Census 1988a, 28). A recent congressional study (Committee on Ways and Means 1985, 7) estimated that if ''the proportion of children in female-headed families had not increased during the past 25 years, ... the number of poor children in 1983 might have been ... 22 percent lower.'' A 22 percent reduction in poverty among children would lower the number by about 3 million.

In summary, women increasingly head households and such households have very high rates of poverty. This is particularly true among minority populations. The poverty that afflicts women has dramatically increased the rate of poverty among children. By the 1980s much of the progress made during the late 1960s and throughout the 1970s in alleviating poverty among children had been reversed.

Public Assistance

Not only are women and their dependent children the largest group of poor in America, they are also the major welfare recipient group (Bureau of the Census 1984, 1–5). Female family heads and their dependents constitute over 80 percent of all AFDC (Aid to Families with Dependent Children) recipients, over half of all Food Stamp households, almost half of the recipients of free or reduced-price school meals, 55 percent of the households receiving Medicaid, and well over half of the nonaged residents of public housing. The problems that increasingly befall women, in other words, impose very significant costs on society.

Nevertheless, as later chapters will detail, most needy female-headed households either do not receive aid or the assistance they do receive does a very poor job of meeting their needs. Most AFDC families remain far below the poverty level and most are still poor when they leave the welfare rolls. This is generally true even when the family receives or has received benefits from more than one welfare program. In addition, many women originally become poor or economically threatened because of deficiencies in public or private-sector policies.

As the chapters here will document, if women and their children are either to be prevented from falling into poverty or to be helped out of it, welfare assistance, other social programs and policies, and benefits extended by private employers will have to be significantly reformed and integrated into a much healthier and more responsive economic system (Chafetz 1984).

The Organization of This Book

The following chapters attempt to dissect the problem of increasing poverty among women and their children. They further detail the growth of poverty in female households; identify its most obvious causes and consequences; critique existing welfare, social, and private-sector programs; evaluate policy alternatives; and put forward some practical nonwelfare and welfare solutions. Chapter 2 begins by providing an empirical analysis of the changes in the poverty population over the last two decades that have produced the feminization of poverty. It addresses the major questions about the feminization of poverty raised in the extant literature and provides an in-depth statistical analysis of the impact of women's poverty on children.

Chapter 3 addresses the question of why women are increasingly the heads of families and delineates the major causes of poverty among women. Chapter 4 shows why welfare programs neither prevent poverty nor adequately meet the needs of poor women and their dependents. Chapter 5 reviews social welfare programs for women in major Western European nations. The intent here is to provide insights into some innovative programs and experiments in other nations that might inform a discussion of reforms of American programs. Finally, chapter 6 discusses nonwelfare and welfare reforms that would ameliorate the growing problem of poverty among women and their dependents.

Chapter 2

The Feminization of Poverty: A Statistical Overview

In this chapter data will be presented to detail, by racial group, the dramatic increase in the proportion of all the poor who are women and children. The data are then used to examine why this change has occurred. The analysis reveals that the key factor in explaining the rising proportion of women and children among all the poor is not the increasing rate of poverty for women and children or, generally speaking, the decreasing rate of poverty for two-parent families.* Instead, it is the huge increase in the number of households headed by women.

Female-headed households suffer a high but steady rate of

---

* An important caveat should be noted. The rate of poverty for all groups is determined by the Social Security Administration's calculation of the official poverty standard. This standard was first calculated in 1965 and then backdated to 1959. Since 1969 the standard has been adjusted yearly according to changes in the Consumer Price Index. The yearly adjustments have been so low that the poverty standard has become an increasingly smaller proportion of median family income. For example, in 1959 the poverty standard for an urban family of four equalled 53 percent of median family income for an urban family of four. By 1980 the ratio for this family size had fallen to 40 percent. Thus, the recent stability of the poverty rate for female-headed families in part reflects the failure of the poverty standard to maintain its historic relationship to median incomes.

poverty. As the proportion of all such households has grown, their high but rather constant rate of poverty has encompassed larger and larger numbers of poor women and children. Poverty, in other words, has become a matter not just of economics, but also of family structure.

The Increase in Poor Female Heads of Households

The number of poor Americans living in female-headed families has increased dramatically since the 1960s (see figure 1.2). In 1960 only 24 percent of all poor families were headed by a woman. By 1987 the percentage had increased to 52 percent. The change has been significant for both white and black families. The 20 percent of all poor white families headed by a female in 1960 rose to 46 percent by 1987. For poor black families, 42 percent were headed by a single woman in 1960, but this had increased to 76 percent by 1987. Women headed about the same proportion of poor Spanish-origin families in 1987 as in 1973—a little over half (Bureau of the Census 1988a, 21–22). Table 2.1 shows the increase between 1959 and 1987 in the number of poor family and nonfamily households (excluding single households) headed by women (Cooney 1979; Cutright 1974; Lantz, Martin, and O'Hara 1977; Sweet 1972). In 1959 the number of poor female family heads was 1.9 million; by 1987 this figure had jumped 90 percent, to 3.6 million.

Both the number and proportion of all the poor living in single, family, and nonfamily female households also increased significantly over the last two decades (see table 2.2). In 1959 there were 10.3 million poor people in female-headed households. By 1987 the number stood at 16.9 million, an increase of 63 percent. About half of the increase occurred in the late 1970s and early 1980s.

The magnitude of these increases is indicated by the fact that in 1960 only 27 percent of all the poor lived in female-headed households. The percentage increased steadily until the mid-1970s, by which time half of all the poor in America lived in female-headed households. In 1978 the percentage reached 52.6, but great in-

Figure 2.1 **Poor Female Heads of Families (in millions)**

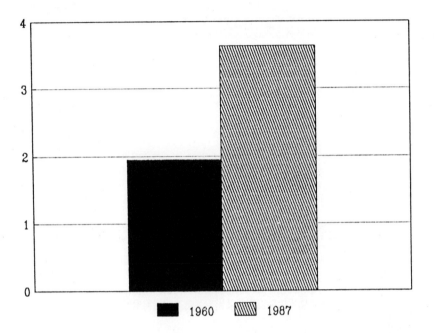

creases in poverty for all household types in the 1980s reduced the
proportion of the poor in female-headed units to 48 percent in
1984. In 1986 and 1987 the proportion of all the poor living in a
female-headed household rose again to 52 percent (see figure 1.2).

Variations by Race

Figures for the poverty rate (the percentage of all people of a given
type living below the poverty line) for members of female-headed
households, broken down by race, are quite revealing (see table
2.2). The rate of poverty for members of female-headed households
actually declined from a high of 50.2 percent in 1959 to 34 percent
in the mid to later 1980s (see footnote on p. 17). (The rate for female
heads of families also declined somewhat in this period; see figure

Table 2.1

Poor Female Family Heads (No Husband Present), by Race

	Total (in 1000s)	Poverty rate	White (in 1000s)	Poverty rate	Black (in 1000s)	Poverty rate	Spanish-origin (in 1000s)	Poverty rate
1987	3,636	34.3	1,930	26.7	1,593	51.8	555	51.8
1986	3,613	34.6	2,041	28.2	1,488	50.1	528	51.2
1985	3,474	34.0	1,950	27.4	1,452	50.5	521	53.1
1984	3,498	34.5	1,878	27.1	1,533	51.7	483	53.4
1983	3,572	35.8	1,935	28.7	1,541	53.7	455	52.9
1982	3,434	36.3	1,813	27.9	1,535	56.2	425	55.4
1981	3,252	34.6	1,814	27.4	1,377	52.9	399	53.2
1980	2,972	32.7	1,609	25.7	1,301	49.4	362	51.3
1979	2,645	30.4	1,350	22.3	1,234	45.4	300	49.2
1978	2,654	31.4	1,391	23.5	1,208	50.6	288	53.1
1977	2,610	31.7	1,400	24.0	1,162	51.0	301	53.6
1976	2,543	33.0	1,379	25.2	1,122	52.2	275	53.1
1975	2,430	32.5	1,394	25.9	1,004	50.1	279	53.6
1974	2,324	32.1	1,289	24.8	1,010	52.2	229	49.6
1973	2,193	32.2	1,190	24.5	974	52.7	211	51.4
1972	2,158	32.7	1,135	24.3	972	53.3		
1971	2,100	33.9	1,191	26.5	879	53.5		
1970	1,951	32.5	1,102	25.0	834	54.3		
1969	1,827	32.7	1,069	25.7	737	53.3		
1968	1,755	32.3	1,021	25.2	706	53.2		
1967	1,774	33.3	1,037	25.9	716	53.2		
1966	1,721	33.1	1,036	25.7	674	56.3		
1965	1,916	33.1	1,196	25.7	n.a.	59.2		
1960	1,955	38.4	1,252	31.0	n.a.			
1959	1,916	42.4	1,233	34.0	551			
Percent increase	90		56		189		163	

Source: Bureau of the Census (1988), "Money Income and Poverty Status of Families and Persons in the United States: 1987," *Current Population Reports*, series P-60, no. 161, pp. 21–22.

Figure 2.2 **Poverty Rate of Female Heads of Families**

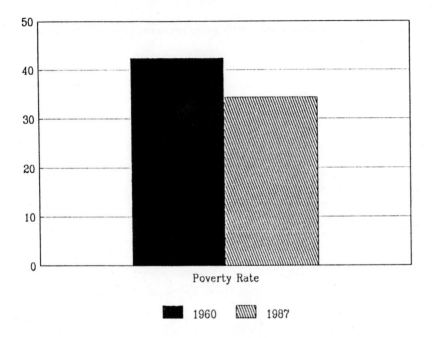

2.2.) During the 1970s the rate of poverty for female-headed households averaged 35 percent, comparable to the average so far during the 1980s. The rate varies considerably, however, by race.

White Poor

White households have the lowest rate of poverty and have had the smallest percentage increase in poverty. These findings should not obscure the fact that the rate of poverty for white female-headed households is still very high (see table 2.2). Between 1970 and 1987, the poverty rate for such households averaged 27.6 percent. The number of poor in white families grew by almost 2.5 million people between 1959 and 1987 (to 9.6 million), an increase of 35 percent. Between 1970 and 1987 an average of 42.5 percent of all white poor

Table 2.2

Poor in Female-headed Households (No Husband Present), by Race

	All persons (in 1000s)	Poverty rate	Percent of all poor	White (in 1000s)	Poverty rate	Percent of all poor	Percent of all white poor
1987	16,912	33.6	52.0	9,598	26.4	29.5	44.8
1986	16,926	34.2	52.0	10,052	27.9	31.0	45.3
1985	16,365	33.5	49.5	9,778	27.3	29.5	42.8
1984	16,440	34.0	48.0	9,570	27.3	28.0	41.0
1983	16,848	36.1	47.4	9,768	28.5	27.5	40.4
1982	16,336	36.2	47.5	9,392	28.7	27.3	39.8
1981	15,738	35.2	49.4	9,347	28.4	29.4	43.4
1980	14,649	33.8	50.0	8,569	27.1	29.3	43.5
1979	13,503	32.0	51.8	7,653	24.9	29.3	44.4
1978	12,880	32.3	52.6	7,262	24.9	29.6	44.6
1977	12,624	32.8	51.5	7,221	25.5	29.2	44.0
1976	12,586	34.4	50.4	7,356	27.3	29.4	44.0
1975	12,268	34.6	47.4	7,324	28.1	28.3	41.2
1974	11,469	33.6	49.0	6,673	26.5	28.5	42.2
1973	11,357	34.9	49.4	6,642	27.9	28.9	43.8
1972	11,587	36.9	47.4	6,682	25.4	27.3	41 2
1971	11,409	38.0	44.6	7,146	32.2	27.9	40.2
1970	11,154	38.2	43.9	6,832	31.4	26.8	39.0
1969	10,412	38.4	43.1	6,531	32.1	27.0	39.2
1968	10,364	38.9	40.8	6,400	32.3	25.2	36.8
1967	10,591	40.6	38.1	6,600	33.9	23.7	34.8
1966	10,250	41.0	35.9	6,511	33.9	22.8	33.7
1965	11,058	46.0	33.3	7,085	38.5	21.3	31.5
1960	10,663	49.5	26.7	7,207	42.3	18.1	25.4
1959	10,390	50.2	26.3	7,115	43.8	18.0	25.0

Percent
increase   62.8   34.9

Source: Bureau of the Census (1988), "Money Income and Poverty Status of Families and Persons in the United States: 1987" (Advance Data from the March 1987 Current Population Survey), *Current Population Reports*, series P-60, no. 161, p. 22.

	Black (in 1000s)	Poverty rate	Percent of all poor	Percent of all black poor	Spanish-origin (in 1000s)	Poverty rate	Percent of all poor	Percent of all Spanish-origin poor
1987	6,842	53.8	21.0	70.6	2,350	53.0	7.2	43.0
1986	6,474	52.9	19.9	71.8	2,261	51.3	7.0	44.2
1985	6,215	51.8	18.8	69.6	2,338	54.2	7.1	44.6
1984	6,462	52.9	19.0	68.0	2,068	54.3	6.0	43.0
1983	6,643	56.0	18.7	67.2	1,944	53.3	5.5	41.9
1982	6,533	57.4	18.9	67.4	1,849	57.4	5.3	42.9
1981	6,081	55.8	19.1	66.3	1,682	54.0	5.3	45.3
1980	5,807	53.1	19.8	67.7	1,501	52.5	5.1	43.0
1979	5,571	52.2	21.4	69.2	1,241	48.9	4.7	42.5
1978	5,392	53.1	22.0	70.7	1,158	53.3	4.7	44.4
1977	5,230	53.9	21.1	67.7	1,204	53.3	4.9	44.6
1976	5,024	54.7	20.1	66.1	1,144	54.3	4.6	41.1
1975	4,784	53.6	18.5	63.4	1,189	55.6	4.6	39.7
1974	4,705	54.3	20.1	65.5	1,012	51.4	4.3	39.3
1973	4,564	55.4	19.9	61.8	917	55.5	4.0	38.7
1972	4,670	57.3	19.1	60.6	822	51.5	3.4	34.0
1971	4,129	55.8	16.1	55.8				
1970	4,213	55.8	16.6	55.8				
1969	3,766	57.8	15.6	53.1				
1968	3,807	58.6	15.0	50.0				
1967	3,892	61.6	14.0	45.8				
1966	3,657	65.2	12.8	41.2				
1959	2,906	70.0	7.3	36.8				

Percent
increase   135   186

Americans lived in female-headed households. Poverty, then, is obviously a very serious problem for white households headed by women.

Black Poor

The figures for black female-headed households are staggering (Bianchi and Farley 1979; McLanahan 1988; National Black Child Development Institute 1983). As table 2.2 demonstrates, the number of poor in such households increased by 135 percent between 1959 and 1987. In 1987, 71 percent of all poor black Americans lived in female-headed households. As with white households, the rate of poverty among black households has not changed significantly. Between 1966 and 1987 the rate of poverty for black female-headed households averaged 55 percent, with only moderate variation.

Spanish-origin Poor

Accurate figures for Spanish-origin citizens have been compiled only since 1972, but available figures are instructive (table 2.2). The number of poor citizens in these female-headed households increased by 186 percent between 1972 and 1987. As with other female-headed households, the rate of poverty changed little (the yearly average was 53.2 percent with modest variations), but the number of poor increased significantly. Between 1980 and 1987 an average of 43.5 percent of all the Spanish-origin poor lived in female-headed households.

Table 2.3 continues this analysis by focusing just on female-headed families (i.e., two or more related persons living together), setting aside nonfamily households and single households. The data reinforce the analysis above. The number of poor in female-headed families increased from 7 million in 1959 to 12 million in 1987, growing steadily between 1969 and 1981 but basically remaining stable since 1982. The numbers increased significantly during the 1970s despite the fact that the poverty rate for female-headed families was not increasing. The poverty rate for female-headed families basically stabilized during the 1970s and 1980s. This again indicates that the number of poor in female-headed families increased rapidly in the 1970s because the base of such families was growing. More female-headed families produced more poor, despite a stabilized poverty rate.

Contrasting tables 2.2 and 2.3 provides another insight into the composition of poverty in female-headed households. Most of the poor in female-headed households are in families. For example, in 1987, 71 percent were in families. This included 62 percent for whites, 85 percent for Spanish origin, and 85 percent for blacks (Bureau of the Census, 1988a: 29). The feminization of poverty, in other words, is mostly the result of increasing poverty among women and their dependent children.

Changes in Poverty Rate, by Race and Sex

Although the data above decidedly show great increases in poor female-headed households, one critical question is not addressed: Could the feminization of poverty be the result of reductions in two-parent or male-headed households living in poverty? In other words, if other types of households have left the poverty ranks, could the number of female-headed households in poverty be the result of their being left behind? Interestingly, the answer varies by race.

White Households

For whites the answer is no. Since 1966 there have not been great reductions in the proportion of white two-parent or male-headed families living in poverty. In 1966 the combined poverty rate for such families was 7.7 percent; in 1987 it was 5.5 percent. Numerically there were 11.8 million poor in such families in 1966, and 9.8 million in 1987. The poverty rate for two-parent families

Table 2.3

Poor in Female-headed Families (No Husband Present), by Race

	All persons (in 1000s)	Poverty rate	Percent of all poor	White (in 1000s)	Poverty rate	Percent of all poor	Percent of white poor
1987	12,076	38.3	37.1	5,918	29.5	18.2	27.6
1986	11,944	38.3	36.9	6,171	30.6	19.1	27.8
1985	11,600	37.6	35.0	5,990	29.8	18.1	26.2
1984	11,831	38.4	35.1	5,866	29.7	17.4	25.5
1983	12,101	40.3	34.1	6,046	31.4	17.0	25.0
1982	11,701	40.6	34.0	5,686	30.9	16.5	24.2
1981	11,051	38.7	34.7	5,600	29.8	17.6	26.0
1980	10,120	36.7	34.6	4,940	28.0	16.9	25.1
1979	9,400	34.9	36.0	4,375	25.2	16.8	25.4
1978	9,269	35.6	37.8	4,371	25.9	17.8	26.9
1977	9,205	36.2	37.5	4,474	26.8	18.1	27.2
1976	9,029	37.3	36.1	4,463	28.0	17.9	26.7
1975	8,846	37.5	34.2	4,577	29.4	17.7	25.7
1974	8,462	36.5	36.2	4,278	27.7	18.3	27.2
1973	8,178	37.5	35.6	4,003	28.0	17.9	26.4
1972	8,114	38.2	33.2	3,770	27.4	15.4	23.3
1971	7,797	38.7	30.5	4,099	30.4	16.0	23.0
1970	7,503	38.1	29.5	3,761	28.4	14.8	21.5
1969	6,879	38.2	28.4	3,577	29.1	19.8	21 5
1968	6,990	38.7	27.3	3,551	29.1	19.0	20.4
1967	6,898	38.8	24.8	3,453	28.5	12.4	18.2
1966	6,861	39.8	24.1	3,646	29.7	12.8	18.9
1965	7,524	46.0	22.7	4,092	35.4	12.3	18.2
1960	7,247	48.9	18.2	4,296	39.0	10.8	15.2
1959	7,014	49.4	17.8	4,232	40.2	10.7	14.8

Source: Bureau of the Census (1988), ''Money Income and Poverty Status of Families and Persons in the United States: 1987'' (Advance Data from the March 1987 Current Population Survey), *Current Population Reports*, series P-60, no. 161, p. 22.

declined modestly during the 1980s (from 5.4 percent to 5.1 percent) while the poverty rate for males with no wife present increased. The number of these families is quite small. There were 223,000 such white families in 1987. In 1978 the poverty rate for white families of this type was 7.3 percent. In 1987 it was 10.3

	Black (in 1000s)	Poverty rate	Percent of all poor	Percent of all black poor	Spanish-origin (in 1000s)	Poverty rate	Percent of all poor	Percent of all Spanish-origin poor
1987	5,797	54.8	17.8	59.9	1,987	55.0	6.1	36.3
1986	5,473	53.8	16.9	60.9	1,921	52.9	5.9	37.5
1985	5,342	53.2	16.1	59.8	1,983	55.7	6.0	37.9
1984	5,666	54.6	16.8	59.7	1,764	56.2	5.2	36.7
1983	5,736	57.0	16.1	58.0	1,672	55.1	4.7	36.0
1982	5,698	58.8	16.6	58.7	1,601	60.1	4.6	37.2
1981	5,222	56.7	16.4	56.9	1,465	55.9	4.6	39.4
1980	4,984	53.4	17.0	58.1	1,319	54.5	4.5	37.8
1979	4,816	53.1	18.5	59.8	1,053	51.2	4.0	36.0
1978	4,712	54.2	19.2	61.8	1,024	56.4	4.2	39.3
1977	4,595	55.3	18.6	59.5	1,077	56.7	4.3	39.9
1976	4,415	55.7	17.7	58.1	1,000	56.6	4.0	35.9
1975	4,168	54.3	16.1	55.2	1,053	57.2	4.1	35.2
1974	4,116	55.0	17.6	57.3	915	53.1	3.9	35.5
1973	4,064	56.5	17.7	55.0	881	57.4	3.8	37.2
1972	4,139	58.1	16.9	53.7				
1971	3,587	56.1	14.0	48.5				
1970	3,656	58.7	14.4	48.4				
1969	3,225	58.2	13.3	45.4				
1968	3,312	58.9	13.0	43.5				
1967	3,362	61.6	12.1	39.6				
1966	3,160	65.3	11.1	35.6				
1959	2,416	70.6	6.1	24.3				

percent (Bureau of the Census 1988a, 7).

The poverty rate for white female-headed households has not changed much over the years (see table 2.2). It was 33.9 percent in 1966 and 26.4 percent in 1987. What has changed is the base of white female-headed households. In 1965 there were 3.9

Table 2.4

Female-headed Households (No Husband Present)

	All F-H households (in 1000s)	Percent of all families	White F-H households (in 1000s)	Percent of all white families	Black F-H households (in 1000s)	Percent of all black families	Spanish-origin F-H households (in 1000s)	Percent of Spanish-origin families
1987	10,608	16.3	7,235	12.9	3,074	42.8	1,072	23.4
1986	10,445	16.2	7,227	13.0	2,967	41.8	1,032	23.4
1985	10,211	16.1	7,111	12.9	2,874	41.5	980	23.3
1984	10,129	16.0	6,941	12.0	2,964	43.0	905	22.0
1983	9,878	15.9	6,784	12.6	2,874	43.0	810	22.7
1982	9,469	15.4	6,507	12.2	2,734	41.9	767	22.8
1981	9,403	15.4	6,620	12.4	2,605	40.6	750	22.7
1980	9,082	15.1	6,266	11.9	2,634	41.7	706	21.8
1979	8,530	14.6	5,952	11.6	2,430	40.2	570	20.2
1978	8,458	14.6	5,918	11.6	2,390	40.5	570	19.7
1977	8,236	14.4	5,828	11.5	2,277	39.2	542	20.2
1976	7,713	13.6	5,467	10.9	2,151	37.1	561	20.2
1975	7,482	13.3	5,380	10.8	2,004	35.9	517	20.9
1974	7,230	13.0	5,208	10.5	1,934	35.2	522	18.7
1973	6,607	12.2	4,672	9.6	1,822	34.6	462	16.7
1972	6,191	11.6	4,489	9.4	1,642	31.8	386	17.3
1971	5,550	11.1	4,386	9.4	1,506	30.6	355	16.8
1970	5,591	10.8	4,165	9.6	1,382	28.3	329	—
1969	5,439	10.8	4,053	8.9	1,327	28.6	—	—
1965	5,006	10.5	3,882	9.0	1,125	23.7	—	—
1960	4,494	10.0	3,547	8.7	947	22.4	—	—

Source: Bureau of the Census, "Money Income and Poverty Status of Families and Persons in the United States," *Current Population Reports*, series P-60, various years.

million such households. By 1987 there were 7.2 million (see table 2.4). Thus, while the poverty rate for these households has changed little, the rising base has produced a great many more poor white female-headed households: the increase was from 1.2 million in 1959 to 1.9 million in 1987, or 56 percent (table 2.1). Thus, for whites the feminization of poverty is the result of increases in the number of female-headed households, and a persistently high, but rather level, rate of poverty.

Black Households

For blacks, two general factors account for the feminization of poverty. First, there has been a reduction in the poverty rate for black two-parent families. In 1966, 33 percent of all such families were poor. By 1987 the poverty rate for these families had dropped to 12.6 percent. Over this same period the number of poor in black two-parent families decreased by some 50 percent. As with whites, the small group of black male-headed families with no wife present seems to have become poorer in recent years. In 1978 the poverty rate for these 48,000 families was 17.7 percent. By 1987 the number of such families had grown (102,000), and the poverty rate had increased to 24.3 percent (Bureau of the Census 1988a, 7).

During the period 1966 to 1987 the poverty rate for black female-headed households changed significantly (65.2 percent in 1966; 53.8 percent in 1987), but the number of such households increased even more dramatically. In 1960 there were 947,000 black female-headed households; by 1987 there were more than 3 million (table 2.4). In the 1970s alone, the number of black female-headed households doubled. This increase, and a poverty rate averaging over 50 percent, raised the number of poor female family heads from 551,000 in 1959 to 1.5 million in 1987, or 189 percent (see table 2.1). Thus, for black households, the feminization of poverty has been caused by a great increase in female-headed households, a high and persistent rate of poverty for such units, and a reduction in the poverty rate for two-parent black families.

30

Table 2.5

Number of Children Below the Poverty Level by Race of Family Head

	All* (in 1000s)	Pov-erty rate	White family head (in 1000s)	Percent of all poor children†	Pov-erty rate	Black family head (in 1000s)	Percent of all poor children	Pov-erty rate	Spanish-origin family head (in 1000s)	Percent of all poor children	Pov-erty rate
1987	12,435	20.0	7,550	60.1	15.0	4,297	34.5	45.1	2,631	21.1	39.3
1986	12,257	19.8	7,714	62.9	15.3	4,039	32.9	42.7	2,413	19.7	37.1
1985	12,483	20.1	7,838	62.8	15.6	4,057	32.5	43.1	2,512	20.1	39.6
1984	12,929	21.0	8,086	62.5	16.1	4,320	33.4	46.2	2,317	17.9	38.7
1983	13,449	21.8	8,556	63.0	17.0	4,273	31.0	46.2	2,251	16.1	37.7
1982	13,139	21.3	8,282	63.0	16.5	4,388	33.9	47.3	2,117	16.1	38.9
1981	12,068	19.5	7,429	61.5	14.7	4,170	34.5	44.9	1,874	15.3	35.4
1980	11,114	17.9	6,817	61.3	13.4	3,906	35.1	42.1	1,718	15.4	33.0
1979	9,993	16.0	5,909	59.1	11.4	3,745	37.5	40.8	1,505	15.0	27.7
1978	9,722	15.7	5,674	58.4	11.0	3,781	38.9	41.2	1,354	13.9	27.2
1977	10,028	16.0	5,943	59.3	11.4	3,850	38.4	41.6	1,402	14.0	28.0

1976	10,081	15.8	6,034	59.8	11.3	3,758	37.3	40.4	1,424	14.1	30.1
1975	10,882	16.8	6,748	62.0	12.5	3,884	35.7	41.4	1,619	14.8	33.1
1974	9,967	15.1	6,079	60.9	11.0	3,713	37.2	39.6	1,414	14.2	28.6
1973	9,453	14.2	5,462	57.8	9.7	3,822	40.4	40.6	1,364	14.4	27.8
1972	10,082	14.9	5,784	57.4	10.1	4,025	39.9	42.7			
1971	10,344	15.1	6,341	61.3	10.9	3,836	37.1	40.7			
1970	10,235	14.9	6,138	60.0	10.5	3,922	38.3	41.5			
1969	9,501	13.8	5,667	59.6	9.7	3,677	38.7	39.6			
1968	10,739	15.3	6,373	59.3	10.7	4,188	38.9	43.1			
1967	11,427	16.3	6,729	58.8	11.3	4,558	39.9	47.4			
1966	12,146	17.4	7,204	59.3	12.1	4,774	39.3	50.6			
1965	14,388	20.7	8,595	59.7	14.4	5,022	35.0	65.5			
1960	17,288	26.5	11,299	64.9	20.0						
1959	17,208	26.9	11,386	66.1	20.6						

Source: Bureau of the Census (1988), "Money Income and Poverty Status of Families and Persons in the United States: 1987," *Current Population Reports*, series P-60, no. 161, p. 21.

*Includes all related children under 18.

†Percentages do not add up to 100 because children of Spanish origin can be of any race.

Spanish-origin Households

Among Spanish-origin households, poverty has increased for all family types, and there has been a significant growth in female-headed households. The increase in poverty has been caused by a rise in the number of families, rather than by increases in the rate of poverty. The rate of poverty has remained high but steady, while the number of Spanish-origin families has grown. In 1973 the poverty rate for two-parent and male-headed families was 13.1 percent; in 1987 it was 17.9 percent. There were 1.5 million poor in such families in 1972 and 2.8 million in 1987 (Bureau of the Census 1988a, 7). The poverty rate for Spanish-origin female-headed households did not change markedly (51.5 percent in 1972: 51.8 percent in 1987), but the number of these households increased significantly. In 1971 there were 329,000 female-headed households (see table 2.4); by 1987 the number had risen by 225 percent to 1.1 million. The 211,000 poor Spanish-origin families headed by a woman in 1973 expanded to 555,000 by 1987, an increase of 163 percent (see table 2.1). Thus, Spanish-origin households of all types have suffered increases in poverty. The number of female-headed households has increased significantly, and their rate of poverty is even higher than for other Spanish-origin households.

Summary: The Causes of the Feminization of Poverty, by Race

The feminization of poverty has in considerable measure resulted from large increases in the number of female household heads, and a high and basically steady rate of poverty for such families. Decreases in the poverty rate of black two-parent families have also contributed to the predominance of families headed by women among the black poverty population.

At present, over half of all the poor in America live in households headed by single women. As we will detail below, a majority of all poor children in America live in these female-headed families.

Figure 2.3 **Percentage of Poor Children by Race, 1987**

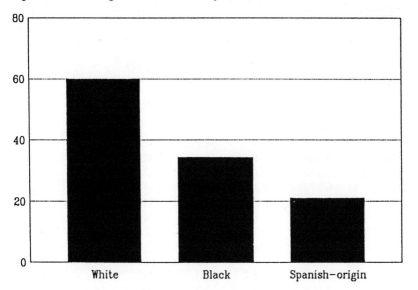

The Impact of Women's Poverty on Children

Poverty among children has been increasing quite significantly since the early 1970s. There have been more poor children in the 1980s (an average of 12.5 million) than in any period since the early to mid-1960s (see table 2.5). The number of poor children increased by over 3 million in the short period between 1979 and 1984. This was true despite a decrease of 9 million in the total population of children between 1968 and 1983. Between 1982 and 1987 the poverty rate for children averaged 20.5 percent. This was the highest rate of poverty among children since the early 1960s.

Breaking the figures down by race yields some interesting insights. As table 2.5 and figure 2.3 show, the majority of all poor children are white. In 1987, 60.1 percent of all poor children were white, about the same percentage as during the 1960s and 1970s. The poverty rate for white children has averaged 15.4 percent. This

Table 2.6

Poor Children in Female-headed Families (No Husband Present)

	Number	Percent of all poor children	Poverty rate	Number of white poor children (in 1000s)	Percent of white poor children	Poverty rate
1987	7,074	56.9	54.7	3,474	46.0	45.8
1986	6,943	56.6	54.4	3,522	45.6	46.3
1985	6,716	53.8	53.6	3,372	43.0	45.2
1984	6,772	52.0	54.0	3,377	41.0	45.9
1983	6,758	51.0	55.5	3,399	39.0	47.2
1982	6,696	51.0	56.0	3,249	39.2	46.5
1981	6,305	52.2	52.3	3,120	42.0	47.8
1980	5,866	52.8	50.8	2,813	41.3	41.6
1979	5,635	56.4	48.6	2,629	44.5	38.6
1978	5,687	58.5	50.6	2.627	46.3	39.9
1977	5,658	56.4	50.3	2,693	45.3	40.3
1976	5,583	55.4	52.0	2,713	45.0	42.7
1975	5,597	51.4	52.7	2,813	41.7	44.2
1974	5,361	53.8	51.5	2,683	44.1	42.9
1973	5,171	54.7	52.1	2,461	45.0	42.1
1972	5,094	50.5	52.2	2,273	39.3	41.1
1971	4,850	46.9	53.1	2,452	38.6	44.6
1970	4,689	45.8	53.0	2,247	36.6	43.1
1969	4,247	44.7	54.4	2,068	36.5	45.2
1968	4,409	41.0	55.2	2,075	32.5	44.4
1967	4,246	37.1	54.3	1,930	28.7	42.1
1966	4,262	35.0	58.2	2,112	29.3	46.9
1965	4,562	31.7	64.2	2,321	26.9	52.9
1960	4,095	23.7	68.4	2,357	21.0	59.9
1959	4,145	24.1	72.2	2,420	21.2	64.6
Percent increase	71.0				43.0	

Source: Bureau of the Census (1985), "Money Income and Poverty Status of Families and Persons in the United States: 1984" (Advance Data from the March 1985 Current Population Survey), *Current Population Reports*, series P-60, no. 149, pp. 21–23.

	Number of black poor children (in 1000s)	Percent of black poor children	Poverty rate	Number of Spanish-origin poor children (in 1000s)	Percent of Spanish origin poor children	Poverty rate
1987	3,394	79.0	68.3	1,241	47.2	70.1
1986	3,251	80.4	67.1	1,194	49.5	66.7
1985	3,181	78.4	66.9	1,247	49.6	72.4
1984	3,234	74.8	66.0	1,093	47.2	71.0
1983	3,187	74.6	68.3	1,018	45.2	70.6
1982	3,269	74.5	70.7	990	46.8	71.8
1981	3,051	73.2	67.7	909	48.5	67.3
1980	2,944	75.4	64.8	809	47.1	65.0
1979	2,887	77.1	63.1	668	44.4	62.2
1978	2,948	78.0	66.4	663	44.0	68.9
1977	2,885	74.9	65.7	686	48.9	68.6
1976	2,778	73.9	65.6	636	44.7	67.3
1975	2,724	70.1	66.0	694	42.9	68.4
1974	2,651	71.4	65.0	621	43.9	64.3
1973	2,635	68.9	67.2	606	44.4	68.7
1972	2,686	66.7	69.5			
1971	2,329	60.7	66.6			
1970	2,383	60.7	67.7			
1969	2,137	58.1	68.2			
1968	2,241	54.1	70.5			
1967	2,265	49.1	72.4			
1966	2,107	44.1	76.6			
1959	1,475	29.4	81.6			

| Percent increase | 130.0 | | | 105.0 | | |

is the highest rate of poverty for white children since the early 1960s and a significant increase over the 1970s, when the rate averaged 11 percent.

Poverty among black children has also increased modestly since the early 1970s. In 1987 there were 4.3 million poor black children. This was slightly less than the 4.4 million black children who were poor in 1982, but higher than most years during the 1970s. The rate of poverty for black children in 1987 was 45.1 percent, an increase over the rates that prevailed during the 1970s when an average of 41 percent of all black children were poor. The rate of poverty for black children is three times the rate for white children.

Figures for Spanish-origin children have only been available since 1973, but they show that poverty among children in these families has also been increasing. The poverty rate for Spanish-origin children increased from 27.8 percent in 1973 to 39.3 percent in 1987.

The data in table 2.6 strongly suggest that the increase in female-headed families has played a major role in the increase in poverty among children (see also figure 1.5). Over half of all poor children in America now live in female-headed families, compared with less than 25 percent in the late 1950s and early 1960s. By the 1970s an average of 53 percent of all the poor children in America lived in families headed by single women, with a high of 58.5 percent in 1978. The average for 1980–1987 was 53.0 percent. The poverty rate for children in female-headed households has remained over 50 percent in every year since 1959 except one (in 1979 it was 48.6 percent) (Bureau of the Census 1988a, 21).

As noted in chapter 1, a 1985 congressional study estimated by means of a statistical simulation that the number of poor children in 1983 might have been almost 3 million, or 22 percent lower, had the proportion of children living in female-headed families not increased (Ways and Means 1985, 7). Chapter 3 provides additional empirical evidence that increasing poverty among American children is directly related to the growth in female-headed families.

Figure 2.4 **Poverty Rates of Children, by Family Type, 1987**

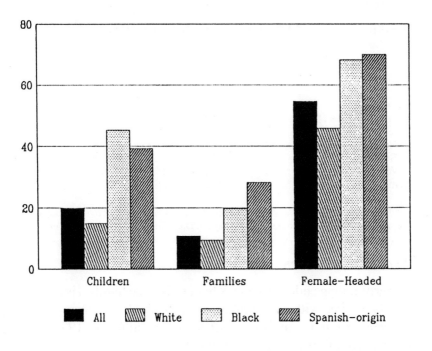

Poor White Children

The data in table 2.6 show the severity of poverty for children in both white and minority female-headed families. Between 1959 and 1987 the number of poor white children in female-headed families increased by 43 percent, from 2.4 million to 3.5 million. The rate of poverty for children in these families averaged 41.9 percent during the 1970s, climbing to 45.8 percent in 1987. During the 1970s more than 40 percent of all poor white children lived in female-headed families. Because of significant increases during the early 1980s in rates of poverty for white male-headed families, the percentage dropped to 39.2 percent in 1982 and 39.0 percent in 1983, but then rose to 46 percent in 1987.

Table 2.7

Poverty Rates per 100 Children by Family Type and Race, 1983

Children	Black	White	Spanish-origin	All children under 18 years
Total	46.7	17.3	38.2	22.2
In female-headed families (total)	68.5	47.6	70.5	55.8
Mothers:				
Never married	77.2	71.3	85.8	75.1
Separated or divorced	66.8	47.3	70.1	53.5
Widowed	60.7	27.9	38.9	41.1
In male-present families	23.8	11.9	27.3	13.5

Source: Committee on Ways and Means (1985), *Children in Poverty*, House of Representatives, 99th Congress (Washington, D.C.: GPO).

Poor Black Children

Poverty among children in black female-headed families is considerably worse, with the number of such children rising by 130 percent—from 1.5 million in 1959 to 3.4 million in 1987. The percentage of all poor black children who live in female-headed families increased steadily from the late 1950s, stabilizing in the mid- to high 70s percentage range in recent years. In 1987 almost one out of every two black children in America lived in poverty, and 79 percent of these children lived in female-headed families. The poverty rate for children in black female-headed families averaged 66.8 percent between 1970 and 1987. In 1987 the poverty rate was still 68.3 percent. These figures are particularly ominous since the data show that three out of four black children can expect to spend some of their childhood in a single-parent family (Bumpass and Rindfuss 1979, 53). The overwhelming majority of all black single-parent families are female-headed.

Poor Spanish-origin Children

The data for Spanish-origin children reveal a slightly different picture. While the number of poor children in female-headed families has increased significantly, their percentage of the Span-ish-origin poor has not. This suggests that poverty has risen signif-icantly for both male- and female-headed Spanish-origin families. Between 1973 and 1987, an average of 46.2 percent of all poor Spanish-origin children lived in female-headed households, with only modest yearly variation. The poverty rate for children in these female-headed families, however, is very high. During the 1980s an average of 69.4 percent of all children in families headed by a Spanish-origin woman lived in poverty.

Figure 2.4 graphically reveals how strikingly at variance rates of poverty are for children of different races and in various types of families. Children in general suffer high rates of poverty when compared with other groups in our society, but those in intact families have much lower rates of poverty than do those in families headed by a single woman. All children, regardless of race, suffer very high rates of poverty when they live only with their mother. The poverty rates for Spanish-origin and black children in female-headed families are particularly severe. Table 2.7 breaks down the poverty rates for children according to whether the female family head has ever been married, and, if so, how the marriage ended. The highest rates of poverty are suffered by children of women who have never been married. Over 70 percent of all the chil-dren in such families are poor, reaching almost 86 percent for Spanish-origin children. Children of widows, especially white and Spanish-origin children, suffer the lowest rates of poverty.

Conclusions

The data presented show the changes in poverty demographics that have resulted in women and their dependent children becoming an increasingly large proportion of all the official poor in America. At present over half of all the poor in America live in female-headed households. More than half of all the poor children in America live in homes headed by single women, including almost 80 percent of all poor black children.

The rate of poverty for female-headed households has always been high, and it has not changed dramatically over the last fifteen years (see the caveat in the footnote on p. 17). What has changed is the number of female-headed households. As this type of household has increased, the high rate of poverty experienced by this type of family unit has greatly increased the number of poor women and children. Chapter 3 presents a statistical analysis that lends weight to these conclusions.

Chapter 3

Female-headed Households: Growth and Poverty

This chapter first seeks to explain why an increasingly large proportion of American households are headed by women. The professional literature is then reviewed to provide insights into why a disproportionate percentage of all female-headed households are poor. Finally, an empirical analysis is carried out to isolate statistically the antecedents of poverty among female-headed households.

The Increase in Female Heads of Households

One of the obvious questions raised by the analysis in chapter 2 is why has the number of female household heads increased so dramatically? There is a considerable literature on this topic (Cooney 1979; Cutright 1974; Korbin 1973; Lantz, Martin, and O'Hara 1977; Ross and Sawhill 1975). Controlling for population growth, the research shows that the increase in female-headed households has resulted from an aging population with more widows, greatly increased rates of divorce and separation, later marriages and less remarriage, and higher rates of out-of-wedlock births. Differing methodologies give each of these factors a somewhat dissimilar weight, but all conclude that women are now much more likely than they were in the past to form independent households (Ways and Means 1985, 66).

Mortality and Marriage Rates

Among older women, the increase in household heads in part reflects the differences in male and female mortality. Life expectancy of women at 65 exceeds that of men by 4.5 years (National Center for Health Statistics 1982, table 3). Older women who become single increasingly elect to maintain their own households rather than live with others. Widowed women are less likely than widowed men to remarry (Bureau of the Census 1976, table C). Since 1980 more than half of all women over 65 have maintained a private residence.

The increase in female household heads among younger women is the product of later marriages, a higher divorce and separation rate, an increase in single parenting, and less hesitation about living away from parents. Younger women are now on average marrying some two years later than they did in the 1950s (Cherlin 1980). In 1950 the average age of first marriage was 20.3; in 1984 it was 22.8. In 1950 only about one-fourth of all 20 to 24-year-old women had never been married. By 1986 the proportion had risen to 57.9 percent (Bureau of the Census 1987, table 49).

Divorce and Separation

Divorce and separation have increased dramatically over the same period (Bane 1976; Cherlin 1981; Clayton and Voss 1977; Glick and Spanier 1980; Lasch 1980; Moore and Waite 1981). The number of divorced persons per 1,000 active marriages increased from 35 in 1960 to 130 in 1987. The rate for women and minorities is even higher (see table 3.1).

The data, perhaps deceptive since they do not control for income level and age of first marriage, nonetheless suggest that black

Table 3.1

Divorce Rates, 1960-1987 (per 1000 marriages)

	Men			Women	
	White	Black		White	Black
1960	27	45	1960	38	78
1970	32	62	1970	56	104
1975	51	96	1975	77	178
1979	66	152	1979	102	243
1980	74	149	1980	110	258
1982	86	176	1982	128	265
1986	102	166	1986	145	332
1987	102	184	1987	142	317

Source: Bureau of the Census (1989), *Statistical Abstract of the United States 1989*, 109th ed. (Washington D.C.: GPO), table 53, p. 43.

women have a much higher rate of divorce than any other group. In simple numerical terms, the rate of divorce for black women is more than twice the rate for white women. Black women are also much more likely to be separated from their husband, and separations have been increasing. In 1960, 12.4 percent of all black women and 1.7 percent of all white women reported being separated (Bureau of the Census 1981c, 39). By 1986, the figures were 15.2 percent and 3.3 percent, respectively.

Divorce and separation, then, have increased greatly since the 1960s, especially for black women. The early 1970s were the first years in American history when more marriages ended in divorce than in death. Cherlin (1981, 23) estimates that almost one-half of the marriages that took place in the 1970s will end in divorce. When divorce occurs, remarriage is now less likely. The remarriage rate for women age 25 to 44 declined 33 percent between 1970 and 1987.

Out-of-wedlock Births

Another factor that has significantly contributed to the increase in female-headed families is out-of-wedlock births (Furstenberg

1976; Furstenberg, Lincoln, and Menken 1981; Hofferth and Moore 1979; Moore and Burt 1981; Moore and Caldwell 1976; Scharf 1979; Vinovskis 1981). Since 1950 such births have increased almost sixfold, rising from 142,000 in 1950 to 828,200 in 1985 (Bureau of the Census, 1987, table 52). The raw data show that unmarried black women have children at a much higher rate than do unmarried white women. Research by Pittman (Select Committee on Children, Youth, and Families [SCCYF] 1983b, 122) shows that "black teenagers are 1.5 times more likely to get pregnant, 3.5 times more likely to give birth and 5.5 times more likely to be unmarried parents." Still, race may not be an independent predictor. Young women from low-income families—regardless of race—are much more likely to become pregnant while still teenagers. White teenagers who become pregnant are more likely than black teenagers to obtain an abortion or marry before the birth of the child (Furstenberg, Lincoln, and Menken 1981, 17–31).

While births to unmarried women have increased, births to married women have declined. The result is that a growing proportion of all children are born out of wedlock. In 1950, 4 percent of all children were born to unwed mothers; by 1985, this figure was 22 percent. The increase is far greater for black women. In 1985, 60.1 percent of all black children born in America had an unmarried mother, whereas only 14.5 percent of all white children had an unwed mother (Bureau of the Census 1987, table 87).

Often these figures represent striking changes in a very short period of time. As recently as 1970, only 29.5 percent of all black children lived in a family headed by a divorced, separated, single, or widowed mother. By 1986, 50.6 percent of all black children lived in this type of family. The contrast with white and Spanish-origin families is stark. In 1986, only 27.7 percent of all Spanish-origin children lived in a female-headed family with no father present. About 16 percent of all white children lived in this type of household (Bureau of the Census 1987, table 69).

The percentage of all single-parent families headed by a woman who has never been married has also increased significantly. In 1970 only 1 percent of single mothers had never been married. The figure in 1986 was 6.7 percent. Among black women the percentage increased from 5 percent in 1970 to 28.4 percent in 1986. Among whites it grew ninefold, to 3.2 percent.

There is a growing literature that concludes that single parenting and divorce and separation rates correlate significantly with demographic and economic variables (Guttentag and Secord 1983, 199–230). When the number of available women significantly outnumbers that of available men, illegitimacy and marital disruption increase. This is a particularly significant problem for the black population. In the United States in general, and more acutely in some major urban areas, young black women greatly outnumber young black men (Guttentag and Secord 1983, 214; Jackson 1973, 23). Infant mortality rates, teenage mortality rates, and military service seem to contribute to the unbalanced sex ratios. Poor men, regardless of race, are also less likely to marry and support a family. Young black men suffer particularly high unemployment rates and are thus less able to support a family.

The factors reviewed here seem to be the major contributors to the growth of female households. But why do female householders suffer such a high rate of poverty?

Antecedents of Female-household Poverty

Studies have isolated many of the facts that combine to produce high rates of poverty among female households. This section discusses some of the major variables and assesses their predictive insights.

Lack of Adequate Child Support

One of the most obvious factors contributing to the poverty of female-headed families is the low level of child support by absent fathers (Bureau of the Census 1980a). In recent years on average

Table 3.2

Women Seeking Child Support, by Race, 1985

Race	Number (in millions)	Percent awarded support	Percent receiving support	Mean annual support (in dollars)
All women				
White	6.3	71.0	43.0	2,294
Black	2.3	36.0	20.4	1,754
Spanish-origin	0.813	42.0	23.6	2,011
Women below the poverty level seeking support				
White	1.6	50.0	26.0	1,463
Black	1.2	27.0	15.0	1,085
Spanish-origin	0.414	24.0	10.4	—

Source: Bureau of the Census (1987), *Statistical Abstract of the United States 1988*, 108th ed. (Washington, D.C.: GPO), table 597.

only some 35 percent of all women with minor children from an absent father have received child support, and of these, only about 68 percent have received the agreed upon amount (SCCYF 1983b, 20). Figures for 1985 provide examples from a typical year. In 1985 there were 8.8 million women with children from an absent father. Sixty-one percent of these women were awarded child support but only 37 percent actually received support payments. These payments averaged $2,215 annually. Thus, most mothers did not receive any support, and those who did tended to receive only modest amounts.

White women generally receive more support than do minority women. The data in table 3.2 (which do not control for the socio-economic status of the father) suggest considerable variance in support by race. None of the family types received decent levels of financial support, but white women were more often awarded support and were more likely to receive the support awarded. Only 36 percent of black women were awarded support, and only 20.4 percent actually received any payments. The situation was little better for women of Spanish origin. Given these data, it is not surprising that studies show that men tend to be better off financially after a divorce, whereas women tend to end up in worse financial condition (Espenshade 1979; Weitzman 1980).

Women below the poverty level are even less likely to be awarded or receive child support. Only 40 percent of all women living in poverty are awarded support and only 21 percent received any payments in 1985. Black and Spanish-origin mothers were even less likely to be awarded support or benefit from payments. Among all poor women the mean annual payment received was only $1,383.

The low level of financial support by minority men obviously has a financial antecedent. Several studies have shown that low-income black males have conventional attitudes toward marriage and family life, but high rates of unemployment and limited income make it difficult for them to be stable providers and marriage partners (Levy 1980, 42–46; Ross and Sawhill 1975,74, 86). Young black men have higher rates of unemployment than any other group. In 1986, 23.5 percent of all black males 20 to 24 years of age were unemployed. Among 16- to 19-year-olds the rate was 39.3 percent, and for 25- to 34-year-olds it was 13.5 percent.

Fertility Rates

Fertility rates also seem to contribute to poverty. The more children a woman has to support, the more likely the family is to be poor (Bureau of the Census 1988a, 37). In 1987, for example, 33.6 percent of all female household heads with one child were poor; these rates rose to 69 percent of those with three children, and 78 percent of those with four children. The poverty rates for minority women were even higher. Sixty percent of all black female family heads with two children lived in poverty.

Minority women have the highest fertility rates, but the differences between the races have narrowed as fertility rates have dropped for all women. The 1950 fertility rate of 106 children per

1,000 women, for example had dropped to 66 by 1985. As late as 1970 the difference between the races was major: white women had a fertility rate of 84, compared with 115 for black women. In 1985 the rate for white women was 63, compared with 82 for black women.

Fertility rates also seem to contribute to poverty in several other ways. First, the younger a woman is when she has children, the more children she is likely to have. The more children a woman has, the less likely she is to be able to support them. Additionally, about 80 percent of teenage mothers never complete high school. Thus, teenage mothers suffer earning handicaps that generally last a lifetime. Minority women tend both to have children earlier and to have more children (Bureau of the Census 1987, 37). Women with two or more children have lower rates of employment, lower employment and career aspirations, and lower wage earnings (Carlson and Stinson 1982; Cramer 1980; Smith-Loving and Tickamyer 1978; Smith-Loving and Tickamyer 1982).

Employment and Wages

The economic condition of female household heads is also affected by a series of problems related to employment and wage earnings (Chafetz 1984, 47–79). Most obviously, unemployment rates for poor female family heads are very high (Bureau of the Census 1987, 37). In 1987, 72 percent of all such women were unemployed. The rate was very high for white women (61.4 percent), but even higher for blacks (83.3 percent).

Studies conducted at the Institute for Research on Poverty demonstrated how significantly unemployment rates impact on poor families. The studies revealed that a 10 percent increase in the unemployment rate is associated with about a 2.5 percent increase in the incidence of pre-transfer (before government transfers) poverty. Thus, if unemployment increased from 9 to 10 percent, the number of families with earnings below the poverty level would increase from 20 percent to 20.5 percent, adding over a million new people to the ranks of the poor (SCCYF 1984b, 63).

Even when female family heads are employed, they tend to earn less than male heads of households (Beller 1980; Beller 1982; Burstein 1979; Kessler-Harris 1982; King 1978; Polachek 1979; Rytina 1982; Trieman and Hartmann 1981; U.S. Commission on Civil Rights 1982). In 1987 female family heads had a median income from all sources (i.e., wages, welfare benefits, and child support) of $14,620, compared with $34,700 for married couple families (Bureau of the Census 1987, 4). Minority female family heads had significantly lower median incomes: $9,710 for black family heads and $9,805 for Spanish-origin family heads.

Women workers earn significantly less than male workers for several reasons (Bergman 1989; Fuchs 1989). Many more women work only part time or part of the year. Women also tend to change jobs and move in and out of the work force more often. However, even when women work full time year-round, they earn much less than similarly employed men. In 1987, for example, such women had median earnings of $16,909, compared with $26,008 for their male counterparts (Bureau of the Census 1987, 4). The discrepancy is caused by many factors. First, the mean age of working women is considerably younger than that of male employees (which means that women tend to have less seniority). Second, women employees tend to be concentrated in jobs traditionally considered ''women's work,'' and these jobs usually pay a rather low wage regardless of the skill and training required. Third, there is solid empirical evidence of pay discrimination as recently as the 1970s, and some discrimination may continue (see Bergman 1974; Cocoran and Duncan 1979; Lloyd and Niemi 1979; Suter and Miller 1973; Wolf and Fligstein 1979).

The economic condition of families has also been affected over the last twenty years by the failure of wages to keep up with inflation. Adjusted for inflation, the median income for all families was $30,853 in 1987 compared with $30,820 in 1973 (Bureau of the Census 1988a, 2). Family incomes have been influenced by the increase in female-headed families, the loss of industrial-manufacturing jobs, the increase in the proportion of jobs in lower-paying service sectors, and the increase in involuntary part-time work (Danziger and Gottschalk 1988–1989; Danziger, Gottschalk, and Smolensky 1989).

Welfare Benefits

The combination of unemployment, low wages, and little or no child support leaves millions of female household heads in financial distress. Cash welfare benefits (and Social Security benefits for those who qualify) are generally too modest to alleviate the problem. In 1986, for example, the average monthly AFDC payment to families was $355.04, or $121.05 per recipient (Duvall, Gondreau, and Marsh 1982, 5; Social Security Administration 1988, 335). Many states provided benefits considerably below these averages (see chapter 4). The result is that most female-headed families with no income other than AFDC live below the poverty line. There is also evidence that AFDC rules prompt some families to break up and encourage some women to delay marriage or remarriage (Bahr 1979; Hannan, Tuma, and Groeneveld 1977; Moles 1979). The Reagan administration cut welfare benefits, further increasing the income deficits of female-headed families (see chapter 4).

The Income Deficit

The cumulative result of all the financial calamities that befall poor female-headed families is the rapid increase in their income deficit (see table 3.3). In 1987 the income of the average poor female-headed family was $4,927 below the poverty level for the family size. This was a very substantial increase from 1978, when the deficit averaged $2,483. The deficit is even larger for minority families. Further, the increase in the deficit was most notable under the Reagan administration. The deficit declined or was fairly stable until 1979 but has increased rapidly since then.

Table 3.3

Poor Female-headed Families: Mean Income Deficit

	All	White	Black	Spanish-origin
1987	$4,927	$4,534	$5,429	$5,081
1986	4,688	4,231	5,381	4,884
1985	4,516	4,080	5,084	4,679
1984	4,331	4,027	4,691	4,764
1983	4,269	3,980	4,645	4,581
1982	4,076	3,806	4,219	4,312
1981	3,694	3,289	4,219	3,739
1980	3,216	2,922	3,582	3,248
1979	2,843	2,697	3,008	2,732
1978	2,483	2,251	2,720	2,334
1977	2,239	2,088	2,415	1,962
1976	2,029	1,896	2,180	1,779
1975	2,052	1,890	2,296	
1974	2,097	1,972	2,270	
1973	2,041	1,955	2,136	
1972	2,079	1,930	2,237	
1971	2,138	2,117	2,168	
1970	2,223	2,043	2,451	
1969	2,149	1,979	2,399	
1968	2,338	2,238	2,445	
1967	2,277	2,111	2,511	
1963	2,731	2,527		
1959	2,599	2,447		

Source: Bureau of the Census, "Money Income and Poverty Status of Families and Persons in the United States," *Current Population Reports*, series P-60, various years.

Summary

This review yields many insights into factors associated with high rates of poverty among female-headed households. High rates of unemployment, low wages and income (from all sources), inadequate child support, increased rates of divorce and separation, increases in out-of-wedlock births, and differences in rates of fertility all seem to contribute to poverty. In the section that follows, correlational analysis is used to measure the association between these variables and changes in the number of poor in female-headed households.

Statistical Correlates of Poverty in Female-Headed Households: By Race

The Dependent Variable

The analysis reported in table 3.4 uses number of poor in female-headed households by year as the dependent variable. These data are reported in table 2.2. The analysis was run for all poor female-headed households, and then separately for white and black households. The analysis for Spanish-origin households is not reported because data for such households are often incomplete, and preliminary analysis revealed that there are major differences among the groups that compose the Spanish-origin population (Burke, Gabe, Rimkunas, and Griffith 1985, 29). The Cuban population, for example, is quite different from the Puerto Rican population. Thus, the composite image yielded by group analysis is not very useful.

The analysis also had to be limited to the years in which reliable data for all the independent variables could be obtained, and this varied by racial group. The analysis for all poor female-headed families cover the period 1960 to 1987. For white families the analysis covers 1966 to 1987, and for black families 1972 to 1987.

The Independent Variables

Table 3.4 shows the simple correlations (Pearson's Rs) between the annual number of poor in female-headed households and nine independent variables. The first independent variable is rate of unemployment for female family heads. This variable includes family heads who report themselves to be either unemployed or out of the labor market. The second, third, and fourth variables are designed to measure the income deficiencies of female family heads. The first measure used is the annual size of the income deficit (mean dollars

Table 3.4

Correlates of Female-headed Family Poverty, by Race (Pearson's Rs)

	Poor female-headed families	Poor white F-H families	Poor black F-H families
1. Rate of unemployment	0.21*	0.75	0.40*
2. Income deficit	0.77	0.84	0.74
3. Income gap 1	0.95	0.87	0.99
4. Income gap 2	0.92	0.85	0.74
5. Rate of divorce	0.88	0.66	0.93
6. Out-of-wedlock births	0.91	0.55*	0.93
7. Fertility rate	0.22*	0.05*	0.88
8. Percent of F-H families	0.77	0.66*	0.94
9. Rate of unemployment (men)	0.71	0.11*	0.68

*Not statistically significant. All the other correlations are significant at 0.001 or above level of confidence.

below the poverty level for family size) suffered by poor female-headed families. The second (Income gap 1) is the yearly dollar difference between the median income of two-parent families (the wife may be employed) and female-headed families. The third income variable (Income gap 2) is the yearly dollar difference between the median income of male and female workers. The information needed to construct these variables is reported yearly in the P–60 series of *Current Population Reports*.

The fifth variable is annual rate of divorce. Of several possible measures of divorce, the one used here is divorces per 1,000 married women age 15 and over. The sixth variable is annual number of out-of-wedlock births. The seventh variable is yearly fertility rate. The measure is the number of births per 1,000 women. The eighth variable is the annual percentage of all families headed by a single woman. The data used to generate variables six, seven, and eight are collected by the U.S. National Center for Health Statistics and reported annually or semiannually in *Vital Statistics*.

The last variable is the unemployment rate for males age 16 and over.

Findings: By Race

The measures of association reported in table 3.4 lend support to most of the explanations of female-household poverty discussed above. All three of the income measures correlate significantly with the number of poor in female-headed households. Since aggregate data usually generate high associations, the differences in the magnitudes of the R's are probably not large enough to yield reliable information about which of the measures of income deficiency is the most insightful. What the associations do suggest, however, is that low wages and income (from all sources) and inadequate child support contributes significantly to the problem of poverty among female-headed families.

Number of out-of-wedlock births correlates strongly, but, as expected, the separate analysis by race shows that this is a significant predictor only for black families. Similarly, fertility rate is a significant correlate only for black families.

Unemployment rates for female heads shows a reverse relationship. It is significant only for white households. For blacks, this variable correlates insignificantly because there is much less variance over the years. Rate of divorce is also associated with increasing poverty. As the raw data suggest, divorce is a somewhat more important factor for black than for white women. Increases in the percentage of all households headed by women also correlate with increases in poverty, but this is again a stronger correlate for black households.

One of the most interesting variables is the rate of unemployment for males age 16 and over. Notice that this variable is a significant correlate for all female-headed households, but the racial breakdown shows that it is really important only for black households. This finding seems reasonable since unemployment is so much higher for young black males than for any other group and would seem to render many of them incapable of supporting a family. These high rates of unemployment also seem logically related to the increases in single parenting, and to the high rates of divorce and separation, which we have shown to be related to persistent, even growing, poverty within the black population.

The differences in the levels of association for each racial group suggest that income deficiencies, high levels of unemployment, and increasing rates of divorce are the best predictors of poverty for white families. For black families, out-of-wedlock births, high rates of divorce, income deficiencies, and high rates of unemployment for young men seem particularly important.*

Conclusions

Many factors have contributed to the increase in female-headed households, most importantly the increasing rates of divorce, separation, and single parenting. Regardless of race, female-headed households tend to have low incomes (especially compared with male and two-parent families) and high rates of unemployment. Welfare benefits do not come close to compensating for the income deficiencies of poor female-headed families, and under the Reagan administration benefits were steadily reduced.

There are somewhat different correlates of poverty in black and white female-headed households. Black female-headed households often become the victims of poverty because of high rates of

---

*Many attempts were made to use multiple regression analysis to estimate the collective predictive power of the independent variables. None of these attempts was successful. Separate runs were made for each of the three major groups (all, white, black). Because the income deficiency variables are obviously intercorrelated, a separate run using each of the four income variables (along with the other independent variables) was made for each of the three major groups. This technique limited but did not eliminate serious problems of multicolinearity. The intercorrelations between the remaining independent variables were generally quite high, and too pervasive to be eliminated by selecting variables for exclusion. The Durbin-Watts test did not reveal serial correlation. The R squares produced by the regression analysis were over for each of the three groups regardless of the income deficiency variable used, but the standardized betas were erratic and the standard errors quite large.

divorce, out-of-wedlock births, and fertility, combined with limited sources of income from employment, child support, and social welfare programs. The staggering rate of unemployment suffered by black males correlates strongly with rates of poverty among black female-headed households. A causal relationship between the rates of unemployment among black men and the high rates of divorce, abandonment, and out-of-wedlock births that seem to cause much of the poverty in the black population seems apparent, but it needs to be more rigorously tested.

White female-headed households seem to fall into poverty because of increasing rates of divorce, high rates of unemployment, lower pay, and limited sources of income, including inadequate social welfare services and child support.

Two major problems, then, lie at the heart of increased rates of poverty among women: the first is the nation's continuing high rates of unemployment and subemployment for both men and women, and second is the nation's failure to adapt and expand its social policy to the changing role of women.

Chapter 4

Female-headed Families: The Social Welfare Response

Of all the major Western industrial nations, the United States has always been the laggard in social welfare policy. America's welfare programs are the most recent in origin and the most limited in design, coverage, and cost (OECD 1976, 17; Wilensky 1975, 11). Despite their modesty, American welfare programs rest on very tentative and reluctant public support (Feagin 1975; Shapiro, Patterson, Russell, and Young 1987).

The Positive State

In an insightful article, Furniss and Mitchell (1984) analyzed how social welfare provisions differ among Western industrial nations, and related these differences to the public philosophies that guide the economic and political systems of each nation. Their analysis revealed that each of the major Western nations has a complex public philosophy that defines—and sets limits on—the role of the state in the economic and political systems. To isolate the similarities and differences among nations, Furniss and Mitchell offered a framework for analyzing social welfare systems based on three major criteria: the design and goals of the programs; the political, economic, and social priorities reflected by them; and the impact of the programs on recipients and the political and economic systems. This analytical framework produced four state types: the Positive state, the Social Security state, the Democratic Corporatist state, and the Social Welfare state.

Furniss and Mitchell argue that the American system approximates the Positive state—the least developed form. In the Positive state, welfare policy is primarily a means of social control based on "free market" principles. Social welfare programs are designed to protect holders of property from the difficulties of unregulated markets and from demands for redistribution of income. The authors agree with Wilensky (1975, 109) that the poor in America are given just enough to "defang the revolutionary tiger." The resistance of the American philosophy to social welfare programs is so ingrained, in fact, that only acute crisis has prompted the establishment and most of the expansion of such programs (Katz 1986; Leman 1977; Shram and Turbot 1983).

The Historical Context

Decades after the other major Western industrial nations had begun developing welfare programs, the United States established its first—very limited and modest programs in response to the Great Depression which began in 1929 (Katz 1986; Piven and Cloward 1971, 1979). The economic collapse was so massive that by 1933, one-fourth of the nation's adult men were unemployed, millions of families were losing their homes, and thousands stood in bread lines each day. Millions of those who suffered from the economic crisis were former middle-class citizens who became more and more willing to support radical remedies (Rodgers 1979, 43–72). Still, the government's response was slow. Between 1933 and 1935, President Franklin D. Roosevelt centered his attention on emergency measures such as public works projects and prevention of bank closures.

By 1935 the crisis had deepened. The Works Project Administration (WPA) had provided jobs for millions of U.S. citizens, but some 8 million males were still unemployed. It has been estimated that the WPA provided jobs to only one of every four applicants (Piven and Cloward 1971, 98). Those millions who could not find work, along with the aged, handicapped, and orphans, turned to state and local governments for assistance. Many states, however, could not handle the burden. Some cut the size of grants so that more of the needy could receive some assistance; others abolished all assistance. New Jersey offered the indigent licenses to beg (Piven and Cloward 1971, 109).

The Social Security Act of 1935

The continuing hardship spawned increasingly radical criticism of the Roosevelt administration. Under these pressures, the president launched what historians refer to as the ''second New Deal.'' This New Deal had three primary thrusts. First, the government would use Keynesian economics (to stimulate and, it was hoped, regulate economic cycles). Second, assistance to business was increased to promote an economic recovery. Third, the government established, through the Social Security Act of 1935, assistance programs for those who were outside the labor force.

The Social Security Act consisted of five major titles.
• Title I provided grants to the states for assistance to the aged;
• Title II established the social security system;
• Title III provided grants to the states for the administration of unemployment compensation;
• Title IV established the Aid to Dependent Children (ADC) program;
• Title V provided grants to the states for aid to the blind and disabled.

The Social Security Act created a radical new role for the federal government. Congress previously had subsidized state and local assistance programs, but this was the first time programs had been established that would be run by the federal government (Social

Security) or in partnership with the states (ADC).

As fundamental a departure as the Social Security Act was, its benefits were originally quite modest. Grants under Social Security were extended only to those aged who worked in certain occupations and industries, and payments were delayed until 1942. It was not until 1950 that half the aged received any benefits under the program. The ADC program was sold as a program for widows and their dependent children, and until 1950 only orphans and poor children received assistance. In 1950 the program was changed to Aid to Families with Dependent Children (AFDC), allowing benefits to one parent (normally the mother) in a family with eligible children.

With the passage of the Social Security Act of 1935, the United States became the last major industrial nation to develop a national welfare program—one that was by European standards quite modest. Three features of the act had long-term and significant consequences for U.S. social welfare programs. First, benefits under the various social security titles were designed for only a select category of the needy. Even as social welfare programs expanded greatly in the 1960s and early 1970s, they continued to be categorical rather than universal, as they are in many other nations. The implications of this design feature will be examined in more detail in chapter 5.

Second, some of the social security titles allowed the states to determine who would receive assistance and how much they would receive. As AFDC expanded to become the nation's primary cash assistance program for the needy, this feature remained. As will be detailed below, variations in state participation and payments under AFDC are huge, with some states providing much more generous assistance than others. Titles I and V also allowed a great deal of local autonomy in funding assistance to the aged and blind. Until these titles were superseded in 1974 by the Supplemental Security Income (SSI) program, funding variations by state were substantial.

Last, the Social Security Act did not include health insurance.

By 1935 most other Western industrial nations already had health insurance programs. Roosevelt considered including health insurance in the Social Security Act but eliminated it because opposition from the American Medical Association and southern congressmen was so intense.

State control over the benefit levels under Titles I, II, IV, and V of the Social Security Act substantially limited growth in these programs through the 1950s. In 1960 only 803,000 families were receiving benefits under AFDC, and only 144,000 blind or disabled citizens were receiving assistance under Title V. Thus, by 1960, twenty-five years after the original act, U.S. welfare programs were still extremely modest, and, as events would prove, poverty was very severe.

The Civil Rights Movement

Just as the Great Depression had served as the necessary catalyst for the nation's first major social welfare programs, the civil rights movement and the ghetto riots of the 1960s served as the stimulus for the next substantial expansion of the welfare state. The civil rights movement, which matured in the late 1950s and early 1960s, centered attention on the economic conditions of millions of U.S. citizens. Civil rights workers often charged that many U.S. citizens of all races were ill-housed, ill-clothed, medically neglected, malnourished, and even suffering from hunger. Most of the nation's public leaders simply dismissed the latter suggestion, but slowly the evidence of acute poverty, malnutrition, poverty-related disease, and even starvation began to be documented.

In 1967 the Senate Subcommittee on Employment, Manpower, and Poverty held hearings on U.S. poverty. The testimony of many civil rights leaders contained graphic allegations of acute hunger in the South. This testimony stimulated two liberal members of the subcommittee—Robert Kennedy (D., N.Y.) and Joseph Clark (D., Penn.)—personally to tour the Mississippi delta. They returned to Washington to testify to the presence of severe hunger and malnutrition in the areas they visited.

The subcommittee's initial investigation also had encouraged the Field Foundation to send a team of doctors to Mississippi to investigate the health of children in Head Start programs. The team issued a report documenting extensive poverty, poverty-related diseases, and malnutrition among the children and their families (Kotz 1971, 8–9).

The most dramatic documentation of U.S. poverty was yet to come. In the mid-1960s the Field Foundation and the Citizens' Crusade Against Poverty formed the Citizens' Board of Inquiry into Hunger and Malnutrition in the United States. After on-site investigations and hearings, the Citizens' Board reported its findings in late 1967 and 1968. The findings confirmed the worst suspicions of welfare reform advocates. Investigators had discovered, within the larger population of the United States, a population that might best be described as an underdeveloped nation. They reported "concrete evidence of chronic hunger and malnutrition in every part of the United States where we have held hearings or conducted field trips" (Citizens' Board of Inquiry 1968, iv).

These findings contributed to pressures on Congress for improvements in and expansion of welfare programs. Leaders of the civil rights movement continued to lobby for new programs for the poor; their arguments were bolstered by the outbreak of hundreds of riots in U.S. cities between 1965 and 1969 (Downes 1968). Many saw the riots as evidence of a breakdown of morals in American society and an attack on the nation's institutions (Hahn and Feagin 1970). In the final analysis, however, most members of Congress agreed that expanding social programs would lower tensions and help restore order. Thus, with the cities on fire and media attention focused on the struggles of the black population and the poverty of millions of U.S. citizens, Congress passed major civil rights acts in 1964, 1965, and 1968. It also expanded existing welfare programs and created new ones. The changes included:

• A 1961 amendment to the AFDC title allowing states to provide benefits to two-parent families where both parents were unemployed (less than half the states adopted this option).

• Formal establishment of the Food Stamp program in 1964 (initially, only twenty-two states opted to participate).

• Enactment of the Medicare and Medicaid programs in 1965.

• Adoption by Congress in 1971 of national standards for the Food Stamp program (the program was not extended to all states until 1974).

• Passage of the Supplemental Security Income (SSI) program in 1972, effective in 1974.

By 1975 five new titles had been added to the original Social Security Act, and the original titles had been expanded through amendments.

The 1960s and early 1970s, then, saw the second significant installment in the development of American social welfare programs. It is doubtful that anything short of serious civil strife could have produced such drastic changes.

Systemic and Philosophical Limitations on the Welfare State

Why has the United States lagged behind other major Western industrial nations in the creation of social welfare programs? It is certainly not because the country lacks adequate financial resources, or suffers too heavy a tax burden, or because public needs are less. America is rich, its tax rate is low compared to those in other Western nations, and its rate of poverty is high, both absolutely and comparatively (Rodgers 1982, 1–13). There are, however, at least three major differences between the United States and the other leading Western industrial nations that yield some insights.

The first is philosophical. America has a stronger commitment to individualism and free enterprise than is typical of other Western industrialized nations. The country's two major political parties basically support these principles, and there are no significant third parties that promote other principles. Single-member congressional districts and the electoral college system have the effect of limiting the growth of third parties that might challenge the established public philosophy.

Second, America's fragmented power structure makes the passage of nontraditional and nonincremental public policies very difficult. In the parliamentary systems of Europe, the executive's party or coalition is in control of both the executive branch and the legislative branch, and disciplined parties generally ensure support for the executive's policies. In the United States, by contrast, power is split between the executive and legislative branches, Congress itself is divided into two competing houses, and party membership need not indicate support for the party platform. The result is that it is very difficult to achieve consensus on major policy objectives. Public policy in the United States is generally a short-term compromise between competing interest groups, designed to meet only limited, sometimes conflicting, and almost always incremental goals. Power is so fragmented that small, entrenched groups from the major parties can often veto even modest, incremental policies. Thus, it has generally been the case that only a crisis, or the perception of one, will precipitate significant change in major public policies—even significant incremental change.

Third, in the United States working-class and low-income citizens have less political clout than their counterparts in Western Europe, in part because the Americans are politically less mobilized. The traditional institutions that play such an important role in educating and mobilizing the working-class electorate in Europe, such as labor unions and political parties, are relatively weak in the United States. The result is what Burnham (1980) has called a "hole in the electorate"—the absence of the type of voters who support social welfare programs and left-wing movements in other Western nations.

Characteristics of the American Welfare System

These systemic and philosophical factors have obvious impacts on the design of American welfare programs. Basically, welfare programs in the American system are viewed as a necessary evil. They are necessary to control disorder, and as a paean to the fundamental decency of American society and capitalism. Thus, assistance is given grudgingly, in a form that makes clear that it is charity, and only to those among the poor who are considered the legitimate poor—the aged, some unemployed parents and their children (mostly female-headed families), and the handicapped and disabled. Aid to these groups is means-tested (i.e., based on financial need), designed to be modest, and if possible, temporary. Assistance even to mothers and their children is generally designed not to prevent or end their poverty but to serve as temporary, transitory aid to see the family through a rough period. Under existing programs, the conditions that make the mother poor—lack of job skills, employment, transportation, or child care—receive scant attention.

Since poverty is generally considered to be the result of personal rather than systemic malfunctions, the state of poverty is often considered to be an illegitimate condition. A poor person is suspected of sloth, moral corruption, or personal shortsightedness; and it is feared that aiding those who become poor only encourages such behavior. The economy is thought to be basically sound and dynamic enough to meet the needs of all but the most disabled citizens. Thus, furnishing aid to the healthy poor and their offspring only burdens the economy, keeping it from being as profitable and prosperous as it could be. Welfare programs, then, are essentially seen as parasitic on the economy and unaffordable, especially when economic conditions are particularly bad. It is precisely when poverty is highest that more and more public officials demand the reduction or even termination of welfare assistance. As will be detailed below, the Reagan administration fit this pattern.

The results of the American approach to welfare are obvious. Aid is kept categorical (only specific groups among the poor are given aid), assistance is given as charity (rather than in the universal forms that are common in Europe), and aid is generally given only after a person becomes poor, not before. The result is that poverty in America remains high. Even when benefit levels are raised, as they were in the 1960s and early 1970s, poverty can increase. It persists and even increases because (1) the conditions that make some people poor are not effectively addressed: high rates of unemployment and subemployment, for example, may be tolerated or even encouraged in an effort to lower inflation; (2) those who obtain aid often receive too little to push them over the poverty line (this is particularly true of the nonaged poor); and (3) a large percentage of the poor receive no assistance because they do not fit into one of the categories of the poor who are deemed to be legitimate or ''truly needy.''

With this background, a more in-depth examination of the specific welfare programs available to female heads of households with dependent children may be conducted.

Welfare Programs for Female-headed Families

In one sense female-headed families with children are fortunate, for they are among the categories of people—along with the aged, disabled, and blind—who are considered the ''legitimate'' poor. Consequently, if they fall below federal and state income and asset levels, these families can generally qualify for public assistance. Impoverished nonaged single adults (especially males), nonaged couples (especially those without children), and male-headed families generally have great difficulty in qualifying for any type of assistance except food stamps. Female-headed families with dependent children receive the majority of funds expended by the federal government for means-tested programs.

Impoverished female-headed families may qualify for benefits from several types of programs. Table 4.1 provides an overview of the nation's major social welfare programs. This table shows the basis of eligibility for each program, source of funding, form of aid, and actual or projected expenditures for recent years. The programs can be divided into three types:

• Social insurance programs such as Social Security, Medicare, and unemployment compensation. Social insurance programs are based on employee and/or employer contributions, and benefits are wage related.

• Cash-assistance programs such as AFDC and SSI. These programs are means-tested, with benefits going only to those who meet income and other qualifications.

• In-kind programs such as food stamps and other nutrition programs, housing assistance, and Medicaid, which provide a noncash service. These programs are also means-tested and often have non-income-related qualifications that must be met by recipients.

As the figures in table 4.1 make clear, the three social insurance programs are by far the most expensive of all social welfare programs. Strictly speaking, they are not welfare programs because recipients contribute to them during their working years and receive benefits related to contributions. Female-headed families may receive benefits from these programs as a result of unemployment, or as spouses and children of deceased or disabled workers who had earned coverage.

The two means-tested cash assistance programs are designed for the poor. In fiscal 1986, AFDC and SSI cost the federal and state governments $16.0 billion and $12.8 billion, respectively. The in-kind programs are also designed for the poor. They had a combined total cost of $69.8 billion in 1986, with Medicaid composing 60 percent of these costs. The total projected cost of all three types of programs in fiscal 1986 was $387.3 billion. The social insurance programs are by far the most expensive, followed by in-kind programs, with cash assistance a distant third.

Table 4.2 provides a more comprehensive view of all state and federal expenditures for social welfare programs in selected recent years. These data include state and federal expenditures for the whole range of social services including those listed in table 4.1 plus education, child care, veterans' programs, vocational rehabilitation, and many others. The data again show that the most expensive programs are social insurance, medical programs, and educational expenditures. In 1986 these three types of programs

Table 4.1

Federal and State Expenditures for Selected Social Welfare Programs (in billions of dollars)

Program	Basis of eligibility	Source of income	Form of aid	1980	1981	1982	1983	1984	1985	1986	1987	1988
Social insurance programs												
Social Security	Age, disability, or death of parent or spouse; individual earnings	Federal payroll tax on employers and employees	Cash	103.5	145.0	154.1	138.3	166.9	180.1	194.3	205.6	233.1
Unemployment compensation	Unemployment	State and federal payroll tax on employers	Cash	18.3	19.6	23.8	25.3	16.1	18.3	18.5	19.2	18.3
Medicare	Age or disability	Federal payroll tax on employers and employees	Subsidized health insurance	35.0	39.1	50.4	56.9	62.5	72.2	75.9	79.9	

Cash assistance programs: Means-tested

Program	Eligibility	Source of funds	Type								
Aid to Families with Dependent Children (AFDC)	Certain families with children	Federal, state, local revenues	Cash and service	12.5	7.9	8.0	13.8	14.5	15.2	16.0	
Supplemental Security Income (SSI)	Age or disability	Federal, state revenues	Cash	8.2	7.2	7.9	10.8	11.1	11.8	12.8	13.0

In-kind programs: Means tested

Program	Eligibility	Source of funds	Type								
Medicaid	Persons eligible for AFDC and SSI & medically indigent	Federal, state, local revenues	Subsidized health service	23.3	17.1	17.4	33.4	33.9	37.5	41.0	45.1
Food stamps	Income	Federal revenues	Voucher	9.1	11.4	11.0	12.5	12.3	12.5	12.4	
Public housing	Income	Federal, state, local	Subsidized housing	5.2	7.9	9.1		9.5	10.5	9.5	
Child nutrition	Income	Federal	Free or reduced-price meals	4.8		3.0	5.0	5.2	5.3	5.7	
Women, Infants, Children (WIC)	Mothers with low incomes	Federal	Vouchers			0.9	1.2	1.2	1.2		

Source: Social Security Bulletin, Annual Statistical Supplement, 1988.

Table 4.2

Percent of Total Social Welfare Expenditure for Selected Programs, by Selected Years

Program	1977	1980	1985	1986
Old-age, survivors', and disability insurance	23.3	23.8	25.8	25.4
Unemployment insurance	4.3	3.7	2.5	2.4
Medicare/Medicaid	11.0	12.7	15.9	16.1
Public aid (other than medical)	9.7	9.0	7.2	7.2
Education	26.0	24.6	22.8	23.2
Total social welfare expenditure (in millions)	$360,602.0	$492,527.7	$730,399.4	$770,521.8
As a percent of Gross National Product	18.6	18.5	18.5	18.4

Source: Ann Kallman Bixby, "Public Social Welfare Expenditures, Fiscal Year 1986." *Social Security Bulletin* (Washington, D.C.: Social Security Administration 1989), 52(2): 32.

constituted 67 percent of total social welfare expenditures. Public aid (excluding medical) composed only 7.2 percent of costs, a decline from 9.7 percent in 1977. As nonmedical public aid has shrunk, the proportion of expenditures going to social insurance and medical programs has grown. Medical program expenditures, in fact, has grown by 46 percent.

Table 4.3 carries this analysis one step further, showing the role of social welfare expenditures in total government expenditures. The data show that social welfare expenditures increased from a total of about 35 percent of all government expenditures in 1950 to a high of 57 percent in 1975, declining to 51.5 percent in 1986. The data also show that while state expenditures have remained fairly steady over this time period, federal outlays increased quite dramatically through the 1960s and 1970s, decreasing somewhat during the 1980s. The Reagan administration reduced social welfare disbursements and raised military outlays,

Table 4.3

Social Welfare Expenditure as a Percent of Government Expenditure

	1950	1960	1965	1970	1975	1980	1983	1984	1985	1986*
Total as percent of all government expenditures	34.7	38.4	42.2	48.2	57.3	56.5	54.6	52.8	51.8	51.5
Federal as percent of all federal expenditures	26.2	28.1	32.6	40.1	53.8	54.3	52.2	50.2	48.6	48.4
State and local as percent of all state and local expenditures†	59.2	60.1	60.4	64.0	63.5	60.8	59.8	58.6	59.0	58.2

Source: Ann Kallman Bixby, "Public Social Welfare Expenditures, Fiscal Year 1986." *Social Security Bulletin* (Washington, D.C.: Social Security Administration, 1989), 52(2): 38.

Note: Social welfare expenditure excludes that part of workers' compensation and temporary disability insurance made through private carriers and self-insured.

*Preliminary estimate

†Excluding federal grants

Table 4.4

Participation in Means-tested and Non-Means-tested Programs

	Female households, no husband present, with children under 18 years	
	Number (in 1000s)	Percent distribution
Total	6,084	100.0
Received benefits from:		
One or more government programs	4,588	75.4
Non-means-tested*		
Social Security or railroad retirement	761	12.5
Unemployment compensation	160	2.6
One or more means-tested programs	3,667	60.3
AFDC or other cash assistance	1,913	31.4
SSI	249	4.1
Food stamps	2,342	38.5
Free or reduced-price school meals	2,362	38.9
Medicaid	2,253	37.0
Public or subsidized rental housing	1,068	17.5

Source: Bureau of the Census (1986), "Economic Characteristics of Households in the United States: Fourth Quarter, 1985." *Current Population Reports*, series P-70, no. 6, pp. 24–25.
*Non-means-tested programs include Social Security, railroad retirement, Medicare, unemployment compensation, workers' compensation, VA compensation, Black Lung benefits, state temporary sickness or disability benefits, foster child care, and educational assistance.

thereby altering the expenditure mix.

A recent study by the Bureau of the Census (1986, 24–25) shows the impact of these expenditures on female-headed households. Table 4.4 shows that of the 6.1 million female-headed households with children and no husband present in 1985, 75 percent received benefits from one or more means-tested or non-means-tested program. Sixty percent received benefits from a means-tested program, and 15 percent participated in a non-means-tested program. Broken down by program, about a third of all the female-headed families received benefits from AFDC, 37 percent had Medicaid coverage, and 39 percent had children receiving free or reduced-price school meals. More than 38 percent received food stamps, and 17.5 percent lived in public or subsidized housing.

Many of the qualifying families receive benefits from more than one program. Ninety percent of the 1.9 million households receiving AFDC or other cash assistance received benefits from two or more means-tested noncash programs, and one-third received benefits from four or more programs. All AFDC families qualify for Medicaid, and many also qualify for food stamps. These families may also be eligible for subsidized housing and reduced-price school meals for their children.

Funding for means-tested programs was reduced substantially under the Reagan administration (Congressional Budget Office [CBO] 1983; Danziger 1982; Danziger and Haveman 1981; Gottschalk 1981; Moffitt and Wolf 1987; SCCYF 1984a, 80). When Reagan's massive tax cuts and huge defense expenditures created a serious revenue shortfall and thus huge deficits, the president convinced Congress that welfare programs had to be cut. Eligibility standards were tightened and funding for many programs was reduced. The result was that between 1980 and 1985, some 4 million people were dropped from means-tested programs. Three million people were dropped from the Food Stamp rolls, while 95 percent of those remaining eligible had their benefits reduced. Some 350,000 families, including 1.5 million children, lost AFDC benefits. Thirty-six states dropped mothers of three with earnings of $5,000 a year or more. Thirteen states set the cutoff level for families of four at $3,000. Three million children lost their eligibility for the school lunch program; almost one million women and children lost their Medicaid coverage.

A congressional study found that real expenditures (adjusted for inflation) for poor children and their guardians dropped substantially between 1973 and 1983 (Ways and Means 1985, 177).

Table 4.5

Aid to Families with Dependent Children (AFDC)

	Average monthly number of recipients (in 1000s)			Amount of payments		
					Monthly average	
	Families	Total	Children	Total (in 1000s)	Family	Recipient
1936	147	534	361	$49,678	$28.15	$7.75
1940	349	1,182	840	133,770	31.98	9.43
1945	259	907	656	149,667	48.18	13.75
1950	644	2,205	1,637	551,653	71.33	17.64
1955	612	2,214	1,673	617,841	84.17	23.26
1960	787	3,005	2,314	1,000,784	105.75	27.75
1961	869	3,354	2,587	1,156,769	110.97	28.74
1962	931	3,676	2,818	1,298,774	116.30	29.44
1963	947	3,876	2,909	1,365,851	120.19	29.36
1964	992	4,118	3,091	1,510,352	126.88	30.57
1965	1,039	4,329	3,256	1,660,186	133.20	31.96
1966	1,088	4,513	3,411	1,863,925	142.83	34.42
1967	1,217	5,014	3,771	2,266,400	155.19	37.67
1968	1,410	5,705	4,275	2,849,298	168.41	41.62

1969	1,698	6,706	4,985	3,563,427	174.89	44.28
1970	2,208	8,466	6,214	4,852,964	183.13	47.77
1971	2,762	10,241	7,434	6,203,528	187.16	50.48
1972	3,049	10,947	7,905	6,909,260	188.87	52.60
1973	3,148	10,949	7,902	7,212,035	190.91	54.89
1974	3,230	10,864	7,822	7,916,563	204.27	60.72
1975	3,498	11,346	8,095	9,210,995	219.44	67.65
1976	3,579	11,304	8,001	10,140,543	236.10	74.75
1977	3,588	11,050	7,773	10,603,820	246.27	79.97
1978	3,522	10,570	7,402	10,730,415	253.89	84.60
1979	3,509	10,312	7,179	11,068,864	262.86	89.45
1980	3,712	10,774	7,419	12,475,245	280.03	96.49
1981	3,835	11,079	7,527	12,981,115	282.04	97.64
1982	3,542	10,358	6,903	12,877,905	303.02	103.60
1983	3,686	10,761	7,098	13,838,202	312.84	107.17
1984	3,714	10,832	7,144	14,504,710	325.46	111.58
1985	3,701	10,855	7,198	15,195,835	342.15	116.65
1986	3,763	11,038	7,334	16,033,074	355.04	121.05

Source: Social Security Bulletin, Annual Statistical Supplement, 1988.

Notes: During the period 1935–1938, a child had to be under age 16 to qualify for AFDC benefits. From 1939 to 1963, a child had to be under age 18 to qualify for AFDC. But for the 16-year period 1964–1980, a child under age 21 meeting the program requirements could qualify for AFDC. Since 1981, a child must be under 18, or 19 at state option, to qualify for AFDC.

Despite the fact that the number of poor children increased by over 30 percent during this period, expenditures, adjusted for inflation, dropped about 6 percent. Funding for all means-tested programs dropped from 13.3 percent in 1980 to about 9 percent in 1988. This represents a decline of about a third in the share of the federal budget going to low-income programs.

Aid to Families with Dependent Children—1935 to 1990

The core cash-welfare program for the poor is AFDC. All states plus the District of Columbia, Puerto Rico, Guam, and the Virgin Islands offer AFDC to one-parent families, with twenty-six states plus the District of Columbia and Guam also offering assistance to some two-parent families under the optional AFDC-UP (Unemployed Parent) program. Primarily, AFDC provides benefits to female-headed households with no husband present. About 80 percent of all AFDC families are headed by the mother, with other relatives of children—grandparents, aunts, uncles—heading another 10–13 percent. Eligibility for AFDC-UP is very restrictive. Less than 6 percent of all AFDC families are two-parent families with an unemployed head (usually male) (Bureau of the Census 1988a, 14).

Table 4.5 provides an overview of the AFDC program, showing the increases in recipients and costs (both state and federal) between 1936 and 1986. The number of recipients grew very slowly until the mid-1960s, then doubled in just five years, and almost doubled again by 1975. Between 1975 and 1986 the number of recipients increased only modestly despite significant increases in the number of female-headed families and the national level of poverty.

Table 4.6 shows the costs of the AFDC program in real (inflation-adjusted) dollars since 1950. The data show that funding for the program has not kept up with inflation. In 1987 the average monthly payment to each AFDC recipient ($125.15) was less than it had been in most of the 1960s and all of the 1970s. The data, in

Table 4.6

**AFDC Average Monthly Payments in Current
and 1987 Dollars, 1950–1987**

	Current dollars	1987 dollars
1950	$20.85	$96.24
1951	22.00	95.80
1952	23.45	101.35
1953	23.20	99.53
1954	23.25	100.49
1955	23.50	101.19
1956	24.80	103.69
1957	25.40	103.21
1958	26.65	106.42
1959	27.30	107.16
1960	28.35	109.78
1961	29.45	113.28
1962	29.30	111.22
1963	29.70	110.92
1964	31.50	116.51
1965	32.85	119.21
1966	36.25	127.15
1967	39.50	134.46
1968	44.75	145.47
1969	45.15	138.20
1970	50.30	145.84
1971	52.30	146.85
1972	54.10	146.90
1973	56.95	142.25
1974	63.37	140.90
1975	69.69	144.90
1976	75.20	149.11
1977	80.08	148.81
1978	83.60	142.50
1979	90.34	135.92
1980	97.10	129.84
1981	103.15	126.63
1982	106.33	125.72
1983	109.93	125.23
1984	114.72	125.72
1985	118.17	124.77
1986	122.09	127.50
1987	125.15	125.15

Source: *Social Security Bulletin, Annual Statistical Supplement,* 1988, p. 100.

fact, show declining recipient benefits of significant proportions over the years. In a recent book Charles Murray (1984) argued that since 1970 poverty has increased, despite increases in welfare benefits and costs. Murray's analysis is flawed, however, by the use of current rather than constant dollars (Danziger and Gottschalk 1985). The constant dollar figures in table 4.6 show that a significant reason for the increases in poverty during the late 1970s and early 1980s was reduced funding for the nation's major cash-welfare program. These reductions meant that millions of newly impoverished families who needed assistance were denied it, while families and individuals receiving aid had their benefits reduced.

In 1988 about 3.7 million families participated in the AFDC program each month (Ways and Means 1985, 192). On average in the 1970s and early 1980s about 70 percent of the recipients were children. The primary reason children become eligible for AFDC is that their fathers are absent from home (84.8 percent) and their mothers cannot support them. Some 21.4 percent of fathers are divorced, 25.5 percent are separated, 33.8 percent were never married to the mother, and 4.1 percent are gone for other reasons. In other cases, children are eligible for AFDC because their father is deceased (2.6 percent), incapacitated (5.9 percent), unemployed (5.9 percent), or their mother is absent (1.6 percent).

AFDC Benefits

There are no standard cash benefits under the AFDC program. Each state determines the financial needs of its poor families and decides how much assistance families will receive (only Alaska pays 100 percent of determined need). The federal government reimburses 50 to 78 percent of a state's AFDC costs (depending on the per capita income of the state) and pays, on average, about 54 percent of all AFDC costs. The federal government sets maximum asset limits for recipients ($1,000), which states may lower. Homes, the equity value of a car up to $1,500 (or a lower state limit), and some items of personal property are generally not counted.

Table 4.7 shows the variations by state in number of AFDC recipients, costs, and average family benefits in 1986. The average monthly benefit to a family was $355.04, or $121.05 per recipient. Notice, however, how much variation there is by state. Two states—Alaska and California—provided average family benefits of more than $500 per month. Eight states, all southern, provide less than $200 per month. Mississippi provides an average monthly family grant of only $116.08. Even in the most generous states benefits are rather modest, and some states seem to make no serious attempt to aid their poor. In thirty states benefits are less than 50 percent of the poverty level. Only in Alaska and Hawaii does the combined value of AFDC and food stamps boost the average family of four over the federal poverty level. In most of the other states the combined value of AFDC and food stamps leaves recipient families far below the poverty level (Ways and Means 1985, 197).

States vary not only in cash benefits to recipients but in the proportion of the poor who are covered. Low-paying states cover a smaller proportion. For example, in a recent year Texas provided AFDC assistance to only 22 percent of its poor children, Georgia covered 39.4 percent, Florida 29.6 percent, Alaska 79.7 percent, and New York 103.8 percent (Subcommittee on Public Assistance 1980, 30–31).

Because of cutbacks, an even smaller proportion of all poor families with children are covered by the AFDC program. During the 1970s an average of 83 percent of all poor families with children under age 18 received AFDC benefits; by 1983, only 62.9 percent received such assistance (Ways and Means 1985, 192). Similarly, during the 1970s an average of over 75 percent of all poor children received AFDC benefits. By 1983 only 53.3 percent were covered by the program (Ways and Means 1985, 212).

The states have always varied in support services for AFDC families. Under federal law the states can provide such services as job training, basic adult education, vocational rehabilitation, family planning, child care, and legal aid (Hanson 1983, 1984). In fact, only a very small percentage of families receive any of these

Table 4.7

AFDC Families, Recipients, and Payments, by State, August 1986

| | Average monthly number of recipients | | | Amount of payments | | |
| | Families | Total | Children | Total (in 1000s) | Monthly average per | |
					Family	Recipient
Total	3,763,252	11,037,797	7,333,801	$16,033,074	$355.04	$121.05
Alabama	49,351	143,920	101,090	67,570	114.10	39.12
Alaska	7,004	17,378	11,128	47,507	565.28	227.82
Arizona	26,910	77,019	53,926	85,319	264.21	92.31
Arkansas	22,761	67,152	47,211	48,731	178.42	60.47
California	570,292	1,659,340	1,110,781	3,640,431	531.95	182.83
Colorado	29,594	84,944	56,890	109,848	309.32	107.76
Connecticut	39,902	116,075	78,385	223,021	465.77	160.11
Delaware	8,132	21,640	14,479	24,666	252.76	94.99
District of Columbia	20,887	54,395	41,410	77,207	308.03	118.28
Florida	98,222	277,355	196,535	267,099	226.61	80.25
Georgia	84,888	241,229	168,379	232,042	227.79	80.16
Guam	1,570	5,590	3,966	3,894	206.71	58.05
Hawaii	14,894	45,864	29,786	71,776	401.60	130.41
Idaho	6,349	17,204	11,536	19,358	254.09	93.77
Illinois	241,774	736,799	493,690	887,150	305.78	100.34
Indiana	54,968	158,686	107,114	145,075	219.94	76.19
Iowa	40,675	126,942	79,500	171,403	351.17	112.52
Kansas	23,841	70,321	46,366	93,763	327.73	111.11
Kentucky	60,171	161,561	108,090	139,506	193.21	71.96
Louisiana	81,619	245,743	172,929	164,207	167.66	55.68
Maine	19,899	57,859	36,074	83,063	347.86	119.64

Maryland	69,107	189,845	123,304	250,399	301.95	109.91
Massachusetts	87,433	235,129	150,623	470,800	448.72	166.86
Michigan	218,905	668,379	428,063	1,246,246	474.42	155.38
Minnesota	54,113	161,226	116,872	329,310	507.14	170.21
Mississippi	54,293	162,764		75,631	116.08	38.72
Missouri	66,740	201,506	131,582	210,139	262.39	86.90
Montana	8,999	26,343	16,797	37,910	351.05	119.92
Nebraska	16,236	47,440	31,520	61,661	316.49	108.31
Nevada	5,627	16,387	11,106	16,103	238.48	81.89
New Hampshire	4,817	12,655	8,366	19,021	329.06	125.25
New Jersey	119,837	351,202	237,131	502,264	349.27	119.18
New Mexico	18,465	52,706	35,383	52,174	235.47	82.49
New York	366,080	1,094,500	714,613	2,122,670	483.20	161.62
North Carolina	67,156	175,209	118,918	183,564	227.78	87.31
North Dakota	4,929	13,667	9,049	20,323	343.58	123.92
Ohio	227,619	676,001	428,667	809,081	296.21	99.74
Oklahoma	30,807	89,507	61,985	102,785	278.03	95.70
Oregon	30,380	82,125	54,271	120,093	329.41	121.86
Pennsylvania	190,991	580,195	377,182	776,603	338.85	111.54
Puerto Rico	54,148	177,608	120,516	65,864	101.36	30.90
Rhode Island	16,035	44,351	28,679	79,183	411.51	148.78
South Carolina	46,388	131,446	91,619	103,533	185.99	65.64
South Dakota	6,281	17,692	12,221	20,020	265.61	94.30
Tennessee	60,491	165,451	111,859	103,721	142.89	52.24
Texas	141,138	427,236	301,039	289,024	170.65	56.37
Utah	13,750	40,871	26,291	56,267	341.02	114.73
Vermont	7,623	21,862	13,592	40,324	440.83	153.71
Virgin Islands	1,230	4,234	3,145	2,719	184.29	53.52
Virginia	58,252	152,884	102,555	177,915	254.52	96.98
Washington	72,480	203,243	129,424	374,973	431.12	153.75
West Virginia	36,775	115,735	70,052	108,971	246.93	78.46
Wisconsin	98,307	300,017	189,048	584,861	495.78	162.45
Wyoming	4,119	11,367	7,145	16,287	329.47	119.40

Source: Social Security Bulletin, Annual Statistical Supplement, 1988, p. 335.

services. Even job training and placement have never been stressed. Since July 1972, AFDC recipients have been required to register for the Work Incentive Program (WIN). This program was designed to help AFDC family heads obtain job training and viable employment so that they will no longer need welfare. As is detailed below, most states have put little effort into job training or placement programs for AFDC mothers (Ways and Means 1985, 361–367).

Legal assistance to AFDC families has always been oriented toward collecting child support from the absent father. This policy has been emphasized since 1975. As a condition of eligibility, AFDC mothers must assign their child-support rights to the state and cooperate with welfare officials in establishing paternity of a child born outside of marriage. If payments are collected from an absent father, the first $50 a month goes to the mother, with no reduction in AFDC benefits. All additional funds are shared by the federal government and the states to reduce the costs of the program. Most of the states do a very poor job of collecting child support from absent fathers. Nationally, child support is collected for only about one out of five mothers on AFDC. Many states fall considerably below this average (National Forum Foundation 1985).

Problems with the Current AFDC Program

As the major cash-assistance program for the poor in the United States, AFDC is fundamentally flawed. The program plays no meaningful role in preventing poverty, nor does it solve the problems of the overwhelming majority of families that come under its jurisdiction. Most families qualify for the program because of the creation of a female-headed family and receive benefits for less than two years (Bane and Ellwood 1983). The program provides these families with transitional benefits as they deal with a period of poverty. There is, however, a large group of families that remain on AFDC for very long periods. About half of all the recipients of

AFDC remain on the rolls for almost seven years. Almost 25 percent of all the families receive benefits for ten or more years (Ellwood 1986).

Most long-term recipients of AFDC are young, never-married mothers. Ellwood (1986) found that: "The single most powerful predictor of durations, when all else is held constant, is marital status. Almost 40 percent of all women who have never been married when they receive AFDC will have total welfare time of 10 or more years, while less than 15 percent of the divorced women have such long welfare times." The estimated stay for never-married women averages 9.3 years, compared to 4.9 years for divorced women (Ellwood 1986).

Almost all recipients of AFDC remain far below the poverty level during their period of eligibility. In 1983 only 4 percent of all poor families and 3.5 percent of all poor children receiving AFDC and/or other cash grants were lifted over the poverty line by these benefits (Ways and Means 1985, 214).

About 40 percent of those who leave the program remain below the poverty level, and about a third of all families return to the program one or more times (Bane and Ellwood 1983; Levitan, Rein, and Marwick 1972, 50). When AFDC recipients do escape poverty, it is usually through a job independently obtained, by marriage, or by increased support from another family member. A variety of significant deficiencies of the program can be examined in two major groupings: disincentives to work and lack of a family policy.

Employment and Work Disincentives

A major deficiency of AFDC is that it generally does nothing more for recipient families than allow them to subsist below the poverty level. This is true even of chronic, long-term recipients. While the majority of mothers are now in the job market, AFDC mothers overwhelmingly remain at home—unemployed and underskilled. In a highly superficial and ineffective way, AFDC and a number of other social welfare programs emphasize employment. Recipients of AFDC, food stamps, and unemployment insurance, for example, must register for job-training programs and accept available employment or forfeit benefits. About 60 percent of all AFDC mothers are exempt from this requirement because they have children under age six or because there is no WIN project in their community. Another 7 to 10 percent of all AFDC mothers are exempt because of ill health or advanced age. Thus, only about 30 percent of all AFDC mothers are under any requirement to work, unless some of those with children under six voluntarily seek employment, which some do.

But even for those AFDC mothers who attempt to participate in WIN, the program has been a modest success at best. The program has been stymied by a minuscule number of job training slots and very limited funds to provide child care to mothers seeking jobs or training. In the late 1970s and 1980s fewer than 200,000 children a year were provided with temporary care while their mothers received job training or entered employment. While some states have established innovative programs (see chapter 6), most have been discouraged from emphasizing job placement and training because unemployment rates have often been high and because the programs are initially expensive to establish, run, and support. If the programs are to be effective, the participants must be trained for jobs that are in demand, and mothers must be given child support and medical coverage during training and for some period after they obtain employment. The states often find it cheaper in the short run just to dole out modest monthly stipends.

There is considerable evidence that AFDC mothers do want to work and, if given a choice, will choose work over welfare. Some Reagan-initiated changes in AFDC produced one type of evidence to support this conclusion. Until 1969, an AFDC mother lost one dollar in benefits for each dollar earned by employment. This was a 100 percent tax and an obvious disincentive to employment. In 1969 Congress amended AFDC to give mothers an incentive to work. The 1969 rule change allowed an AFDC recipient to exempt the first $30 of earnings, one-third of all additional earnings, and all job-related costs. These provisions lowered the effective tax rate to 67 percent. In 1981 President Reagan convinced Congress to revise the law. Under this revision AFDC mothers were given a standard deduction of $75 for work-related expenses, and the $30 and one-third of earnings exemption could be used only during the first four months of employment.

President Reagan wanted these changes made because he did not believe that welfare programs should be used to subsidize low-income employment. In his view, anyone who could be employed was not "truly needy." The changes affected a very small percentage of all AFDC families. In May 1982 only 5.6 percent of all AFDC families had earnings (Institute for Research on Poverty 1985, 2).

The immediate expectation was that, since the changes would leave working mothers with the same disposable income as non-working mothers and would cause them to forfeit their Medicaid benefits, many AFDC mothers would quit the job market. A considerable number of studies on the impact of the amendments have been conducted (Center for the Study of Social Policy 1984; Cole, Danziger, and Piliavin 1983; Danziger 1984; Fester, Gottschalk, and Jakubson 1984; General Accounting Office [GAO] 1984; Human Resources Administration 1983; Hutchens 1984; Moscovice and Craig 1983), and none found any evidence of job dropout. The studies found that the amendments clearly reduced the AFDC rolls (this, of course, was one of Reagan's intentions), and that the income of those recipients who managed to stay on the rolls was substantially reduced. But women who had been dropped from the AFDC program because of their earnings showed no inclination to quit their jobs, despite the fact that their income declined and they generally lost their coverage under Medicaid.

In the Deficit Reduction Act of 1984 Congress took steps to ameliorate some of the negative consequences of the 1981 amendments. One provision of the act allows the $30 exemption to continue during the first twelve months of employment. Those who lose AFDC benefits because of employment continue to receive Medicaid coverage for nine months, and states may at their discretion extend coverage for another six months (Children's Defense Fund 1984, 1–3).

A second type of evidence that many women prefer work to welfare has been produced by studies of job programs. A number of studies (for a review, see Evanson 1984) have found that female single parents were the most successful clients of the Comprehensive Employment and Training Act (CETA) and the Employment Opportunity Pilot Project (EOPP). The Supported Work Demonstration (described in more detail in chapter 6), which provided AFDC mothers with above minimum-wage jobs and supportive services (child care), also showed real gains for the recipients. Two years after the program the recipients were more inclined than their peers to be in the job market, worked longer hours, and had considerably higher earnings. As Smolensky (1985, 10) points out:

> The gains were particularly large for middle-aged women (aged 36 to 44 at the outset of the demonstration). Only one-third of the women were high school graduates. Fourteen percent had never worked, and 61 percent had not held a full-time job during the preceding two years. Many of these women lost their food stamp and Medicaid benefits along with AFDC, so that only 50 percent of their earnings represented an increase in real income. Clearly, despite substantial disincentives, female heads of households will work if given the opportunity.

Despite this evidence, the Reagan administration manifested limited interest in job programs for the poor. Reagan convinced Congress to make sharp reductions in funding for all job programs (from $13.2 billion in 1979 to $4.0 billion in 1983) and to end funding for CETA. As a substitute he promoted the Community Work Experience Program (CWEP), commonly known as "workfare," and the Job Training Partnership Act (JTPA). Under "workfare," states could require able-bodied heads of AFDC or food-stamp families to perform community service work or be placed in a private-sector job as reimbursement for their benefits. The recipient would not receive a wage; instead, each hour of work would be credited toward benefits received.

The Job Training Partnership Act replaced CETA and abolished public-sector jobs, placing the emphasis on private-sector training programs for economically disadvantaged youths and adults. Two popular programs, Job Corps and the Summer Youth Employment Program, were retained under this act. Less than 200,000 AFDC heads were enrolled in the program in the mid-1980s. By design, the act allows very limited financial support or child care for participants. Given the design and small size of this program, it is unlikely to have a major impact on the employment of disadvantaged mothers. Chapter 6 discusses job programs in more detail.

Lack of a Family Policy

The stop-gap, short-sighted nature of AFDC is no better indicated than by its lack of concern for strengthening the family unit. There is evidence (although it is elusive and controversial) that AFDC rules induce some families to break up and may discourage mothers from marrying the father of their children (Bahr 1979; Becker 1981, 252; Ellwood and Bane 1985, 1–3; Fuchs 1981; Hannan, Tuma, and Groeneveld 1977; Moles 1979; Moore and Caldwell 1977, 166–67; Plotnick 1989; Rank 1989; Ross and Sawhill 1975, 114–120; Vining 1983, 108). The antifamily bias of the program is quite apparent. Two-parent families are ineligible for benefits in half the states. Even in states with a UP program, only a relatively small number of families ever qualify. Thus, a family desperate for assistance might conclude that it cannot stay together. Similarly, a woman might decide against marrying the father of her child (or children) because marriage would make the family ineligible for AFDC or Medicaid.

As will be detailed in chapter 5, in no other Western democracy does the welfare system put families in jeopardy because they are poor. Nor are people required to be poor or, even worse, remain poor in order to obtain or retain most needed assistance (Gilder

1981, 153). In fact, other Western nations have designed policies (often quite elaborate) to strengthen the family unit.

In order to be made profamily, AFDC would have to be available to any two-parent family qualified as poor. Additionally, any qualifying family would have to be given the educational, medical, employment, and housing assistance required to create a positive, supportive environment for the family. The AFDC program falls short on all counts.

Education

Generally, the only method by which mothers can obtain educational services under the auspices of AFDC is through WIN. But, as noted above, the states have shown little interest in running large WIN programs. The result is that the educational needs of AFDC mothers are rarely addressed. Nor does AFDC specifically provide for the educational needs of children. The children in AFDC families may receive some preschool, primary, or secondary assistance, but the program does not require such assistance or help clients obtain it.

The federal government finances about a dozen programs designed to provide poor, educationally deprived, or handicapped children with compensatory educational services (SCCYF 1984c, 115–55). Most of the funds subsidize programs run by public schools; there are special programs for Native Americans, for migrant children, and for bilingual education. Nationwide, only about a million poor and educationally deprived children receive preschool educational assistance and some 5 million primary and secondary students receive compensatory educational services each year, financed in whole or in part by federal revenues. Most of the student recipients are educationally deprived, but they are not necessarily officially poor. The federal government does not collect separate figures on educational assistance for poor children, but given the total number of students served, no more than a third of all poor children could be receiving any special educational attention.

Studies indicate that preschool programs for poor children can enhance their futures. The best known of current preschool programs is Head Start. Established in 1965, Head Start was initially hailed as the most innovative antipoverty strategy on the horizon. It was designed to improve the discipline and educational skills of poor children and to look after their nutritional and health needs. Initially the program was designed to serve 100,000 children during the summer of 1965, but enthusiasm was so high that 561,359 were enrolled, most in hastily assembled programs (Steiner 1976, 30).

Evaluations soon showed that most of the early summer programs were not effective. Certainly the initial expectation that a great deal could be accomplished in only one or two eight-week summer terms was unrealistic. Studies did show that the nutritional and health conditions of Head Start children tended to be considerably better than those of children from similar backgrounds who had not been in the program; but educational gains tended to be small, especially for children who had not participated in year-round programs (Mann 1977). The most critical of the studies, known as the Westinghouse Report, showed worthwhile gains for students in full-year programs, but only minor gains from the eight-week programs—gains that tended to fade as the child completed the first two years of public school (Cicirelli et al. 1977).

The negative reports convinced Congress to phase out most of the summer programs, a task largely accomplished by 1974 (Bureau of the Census 1981c, 359). The conversion to full-year programs and experience-related innovations in teaching techniques led to great improvements in Head Start's impact. More recent studies of Head Start show very positive results (Berrueta-Clement et al. 1984; Yavis 1982, 21–34). After reviewing such studies, Bernard Brown (1977, 9) of the Office of Child Development wrote that the studies provide ''compelling evidence that early intervention works, that the adverse impact of a poverty environment on children can be overcome by appropriate treatment.'' The studies demonstrated that Head Start is very successful in cutting down the rate of school failure, in improving IQ scores and reading skills, and in helping children gain self-confidence. They suggested that the educational gains do not fade, and that a "sleeper effect" often showed up several years after program participation, with Head Start recipients proving more academically competent even into the junior high school years. The more exposure children had to Head Start, the more gains they made and maintained.

Despite the solid evidence that compensatory programs such as Head Start can greatly improve the educational skills of disadvantaged youths, participants in these programs tend to continue to perform below the median level for all students. Educators recognize this gap as the next challenge that must be faced, and they point to inadequate funding as one reason why the programs do not have an even more positive impact.

Funding for Head Start and other preschool programs has remained modest. Between 1975 and 1984 an average of 376,000 children a year were served by Head Start, at an average cost of $704 million a year. By law 90 percent of the children in Head Start programs must be from poverty families. If the unlikely assumption is made that all students enrolled in Head Start in recent years were from poverty families, only about 15 percent of all those qualified for the program by their family's income have been served.

The increasingly positive evaluations of Head Start's impact have restored the program's credibility, and even transformed it into one of Congress's more favored programs. While other social programs were being scaled back in fiscal 1982 and 1983, Congress allocated $912 million for Head Start, about $100 million more than the 1981 allocation. By 1985 and 1986 funding had increased modestly to just over the one billion dollar level. In those years the program enrolled only 448,000 students, a small fraction of the children qualified by poverty. And, in constant dollars, the allocation in 1986 was less than the cost of the program in 1977 (Bureau of the Census 1987, 337).

Health Care

All AFDC recipients qualify for Medicaid, a program established by Congress in 1965. Medicaid is a state-federal program, with varying benefits available to recipients of AFDC and SSI, and, at state option, other medically needy persons. Under the Medicaid program the federal government has established certain basic medical services for AFDC and SSI recipients. If a state will pay for these services for AFDC and SSI recipients, the federal government will share the costs. As with AFDC, the federal government pays 50 to 78 percent of a state's Medicaid costs, depending on the per capita income of the state.

The basic medical services that the states must provide include inpatient hospital services; outpatient services; physician services; laboratory and x-ray services; skilled nursing-facility services for persons over twenty-one; early and periodic screening, diagnosis, and treatment of physical and mental defects in eligible people under twenty-one; family planning services and supplies; and nurse-midwife services. If the state wants to expand the list of basic services and include needy persons who do not receive AFDC or SSI, the federal government will also pay a proportion of these costs. The optional services include private-duty nursing services, dental services, and inpatient psychiatric hospital services for individuals under twenty-one. As a matter of practice, all states with Medicaid programs pay for some medical services beyond the basics required by the federal government. A few states provide all the supplementary services, while some provide only a few.

There is no doubt that Medicaid has had a very positive impact on the health of the poor. Studies (Miller 1975; Silver 1978) show that the poor have considerably fewer untreated medical problems now than they had before the program went into effect. They also show that currently the poor see physicians about as often as other people. Thanks largely to Medicaid and various nutritional programs, infant mortality rates have dropped by more than half since the program was established. In 1965 there were 24.7 deaths per 1,000 live births; in 1986 there were 10.4.

The most serious problem with the Medicaid program is that participation is largely dependent upon a person or family being poor and qualified for participation in the AFDC or SSI program.

But even among the poor, assistance is often not available. In some states 90 percent or more of all the poor can participate; in others, only a small percentage are covered. In 1985 only 40 percent of the nation's poor qualified for assistance under the program. Nationwide, about one-half of all poor children are covered by Medicaid (Bureau of the Census 1987, 349).

Housing

America has never emphasized housing assistance for low-income and poor families. Most of the money spent by the federal government on housing (much of which takes the form of tax breaks) is designed to subsidize the private market, and thus benefits mostly middle-income and wealthy families (CBO 1988; Joint Committee on Taxation 1987; Leichter and Rodgers 1984, 285; Leonard, Dolbeare, Lazere 1989, 33). For example, in 1988 the federal government spent $13.9 billion on housing assistance for low-income citizens. The tax expenditures for housing in the same year cost $55.2 billion (Leonard, Dolbeare, Lazere 1989, 32).

In 1988 programs administered by the Department of Housing and Urban Development provided 4.3 million units of subsidized housing (CBO 1989). This left in excess of seven million low-income families with no housing assistance. The income-qualified but unserved poor population is quite large. In recent congressional testimony (SCCYF 1984b, 71) it was observed that the "poorest of the poor in need of housing assistance number 29 million, including more than 11 million children and 4 million elderly."

About 20 percent of all AFDC families receive housing assistance under one of the government's housing programs (Leichter and Rodgers 1984, 265–87). This means that AFDC families are a bit more fortunate than other types of poor families. It has been estimated that only about eighteen percent of all poor families receive housing assistance (Leonard, Dolbeare, Lazere 1989, 27). Some of the housing that AFDC families do receive is of very poor quality, and much of it is located in undesirable neighborhoods.

These poverty pockets characteristically have high crime rates, poor-quality schools, limited public transportation, and few good jobs.

Nutrition

Almost all AFDC families receive nutrition assistance (Berry 1984). About 82 percent of all AFDC families receive food stamps. The food stamp allocation is based on income and asset limitations. In 1987, qualifying families on average received about $46 worth of stamps per month per recipient or $119 per family. The stamps can be redeemed at retail outlets for food only. Tobacco, alcoholic beverages, wax paper, soap, and other nonfood items cannot be purchased.

Since the Food Stamp program is national in scope and stamp allocations vary with income, until recently some of the inequities of the AFDC program were overcome. Families living in states that pay low AFDC cash benefits could obtain more stamps than could families living in states that pay higher benefits. However, in 1981 Congress voted to allow states to count Food Stamp benefits as income and therefore to lower AFDC cash payments. This policy leaves many families short of the necessary cash to cover housing, transportation, clothing, and other needs.

The Food Stamp allotment, unlike AFDC payments, increases with the cost of living. It is based on the current market cost of foods that meet the Department of Agriculture's nutritional standards and are included in their thrifty food plan. If increases are warranted by market changes, adjustments are made once a year. However, since overall funding for the program has been declining in real terms, assistance per poor recipient has not increased since 1975 (Social Security Administration 1988, 100).

There are two additional nutritional programs for which AFDC families often qualify. In 1986, 48 percent of all AFDC families received free or reduced-price school meals. Under the school meal programs, free meals are provided to children whose family income is less than 130 percent of the poverty level and reduced-price meals are made available to children in families with incomes in the 130 to 185 percent range. The federal government spent about $3.4 billion on school meal programs in 1986, serving about 24 million children.

Sixteen percent of all AFDC families also received benefits under the Supplemental Feeding Program for Women, Infants and Children (WIC) which was established in 1972. This program provides supplemental food to low-income postpartum and nursing mothers and children below the age of six who are diagnosed as being at nutritional risk. Sometimes the families receive supplemental foods but generally they are given vouchers that can be redeemed at retail outlets for specific food items required to meet their nutritional needs—for example, dairy products, cereals, fruits, and vegetables. In the mid-1980s the average monthly benefit to a recipient family was about $36.

The WIC program served 3.5 million women, infants, and children in 1986, at a cost of $1.6 billion. It has been estimated that of those qualified by income for the program, only one-third of the women, one-half of the infants, and one-fifth of the children are served (Ways and Means 1985, 260).

There is solid evidence that the various nutrition programs have had a very positive impact on the health of recipients. Evaluations of the WIC program credit it with reducing the number of children born with low birth weight, a condition linked to birth defects and increased probability of infant mortality (Ways and Means 1985, 260). There is also good evidence that the Food Stamp program has had beneficial effects. In 1977 the Field Foundation sent a team of doctors into the nation's poorest counties to determine if the conditions of the poor had improved since the 1960s. The team reported very significant improvements in the nutrition and health of poor Americans. Most of the poor still lived in inadequate housing and still had far too few resources or opportunities for improvements, but unlike in the 1960s, they were much less often hungry and malnourished: ''The facts of life for Americans living in poverty remain as dark or darker than they were ten years ago. But in the area of food there is a difference. The Food Stamp program, the nutritional component of Head Start, school lunch and breakfast programs, and to a lesser extent the Women-Infant-Children (WIC) feeding programs have made a difference.'' Or, as another Field Foundation doctor said, ''Poverty is rampant but the Food Stamp program brings food into the most terrible situations'' (Kotz 1979, 9).

As positive as the impact of the Food Stamp program has been, some problems still exist. First, some families still do not receive enough vouchers to purchase all the food they need. The modesty of AFDC benefits aggravates this problem. A Congressional Budget Office study (CBO 1977b, 51) estimated that about 57 percent of each food stamp dollar is used to purchase additional food, while 43 percent simply frees money for other family needs. The family could devote a larger percentage of its cash income to food expenditures if AFDC benefits were more adequate.

Second, many poor families find it difficult or impossible to obtain food stamps. Nationally only about half of those eligible for food stamps receive them. The factors that deter recipients are numerous. In rural areas the poor often cannot apply because the food stamp center is too far away, and hours of service may be very limited. In both rural and urban areas millions of very low-income families cannot qualify because of income and asset limitations. The asset limit is set at $2,000 ($3,000 if any member of the household is sixty-five or older); the income limit is the poverty line for the size and type of family. Unless the family's net income is below this level it cannot obtain food stamps. A family can be in serious financial trouble but still be above the poverty line. Additionally, if its gross income is more than 30 percent above the poverty line, a family is automatically disqualified regardless of any disasters (such as the loss of a job) that may befall it.

Finally, food stamp regulations are generally enforced so rigorously as to discourage many poor families who find the endless demands for receipts and documentation to be a form of harassment. An applicant needs at least sixty pieces of information about household income, size, living expenses, and assets to complete the food stamp application. Many applicants find the application and certification process so frustrating and humiliating that they simply abandon their efforts to obtain assistance. The Field Foundation doctors found that an adversary relationship often develops between applicants and case workers who are under pressure to eliminate fraud.

During the early 1980s these problems were compounded by high rates of unemployment and the Reagan-inspired cuts in social programs. The result was evidence of increasing hunger and malnutrition, especially among children and the elderly. Studies submitted to the House Select Committee on Hunger (1985, 25) in May 1985 showed that because of cutbacks in AFDC, food stamps, and the school lunch program, one third of the gains made against hunger and malnutrition in the 1960s and 1970s have been wiped out.

Family Planning

Neither AFDC nor Medicaid places any significant emphasis on family planning. Nor do other federal or state programs even modestly fill in this gap. The consequences are obvious. Of all the Western industrial nations, United States has the highest rate of adolescent pregnancy and abortion. This is true even though the evidence reveals that American teenagers are no more sexually active than their European peers (Jones et al. 1985, 53, 54).

As noted above, there is a well-documented link between single parenting and poverty (especially for women who become mothers while they are teenagers). The link between teenage childbearing and sundry social ills is likewise well documented. ''Numerous studies have shown that early childbearing is associated with poor health outcomes for the young mothers and their infants, diminished educational and employment status, marital instability, and increased likelihood of public welfare utilization'' (Weatherley

1988, 114). One study estimated the 1985 public welfare costs attributable to adolescent childbearing at $16.6 billion (Burt 1986). Another study based on a computer simulation concluded that cutting the rate of teenage pregnancy by half would lead to a 25 percent reduction in the costs of AFDC by 1990 (Wertheimer and Moore 1982, 24). Halving the number of children born to teenagers age eighteen and under would produce a savings of 12 percent.

Despite the obvious link between teenage pregnancy and poverty, family planning is a very controversial issue in the United States, apparently for two reasons. Some conservatives believe that the more teenagers know about sex, the more sexually active they will be. The empirical evidence shows this to be untrue (SCCYF 1984b, 37). Second, the Right-to-Life movement opposes abortion and, in some cases, contraceptives. Family planning agencies provide information about both. However, the evidence indicates that family planning reduces the abortion rate by helping women avoid unwanted pregnancies (Forest, Hermalin, and Henshaw 1981, 109).

The opponents of family planning have managed to keep both the states and the federal government from dealing effectively with the serious problems caused by unwanted and unplanned pregnancies and births. Some modest federal legislation has been passed. Certain family planning services are financed by the Social Services Block Grant, the Maternity and Child Health Block Grant, and Medicaid. However, the major source of family planning funding is Title X of the Public Health Service Act, which provides grants to public or nonprofit agencies that agree to establish and operate family planning clinics. In 1982 and 1983 Congress appropriated only $124 million for such services under Title X. Grants were made to 4,100 clinics nationwide. These clinics tended to be concentrated in about a dozen states. Only seven states have vigorously sought federal funds and have tried to establish at least some fairly comprehensive programs (Weatherley 1985, 18). Weatherley reports only 274 comprehensive programs nationwide. Few of the clinics are located in the South, where teenage pregnancy and childbearing are the most prevalent.

The clinics established under Title X are obligated to provide free services to adolescents and women who are poor. The clinics must offer a broad range of family planning methods and services, including natural family planning methods, infertility services, and services to adolescents. In 1982 the clinics served about 3.3 million persons, about 34 percent of whom were adolescents. Under a 1981 amendment, the clinics are prohibited from providing abortion counseling or referral to teenagers, and they must attempt to discourage teenage sexual activity (Perlman 1984).

A recent study found that over half of all sexually active teens either do not use contraceptives or use them only sporadically. The study also found that most adolescents lacked access to family planning (Hayes 1987, 51). The primary problems identified were lack of adequate funding for programs, a lack of focus on high-risk groups, and poor coordination between programs.

Clearly, federal and state family planning efforts are too modest. Research findings suggest that the Western European industrial countries have much lower rates of adolescent pregnancy and abortion because they provide early and universal sex education, easily available and unstigmatized access to contraceptives and supportive health and income maintenance services (Jones et al. 1985). These services, as part of a coordinated package of social policies, could play a very significant role in reducing poverty in the United States.

Conclusions

The social welfare programs available to impoverished women and their dependents are seriously flawed. The programs, individually and collectively, are not designed to prevent poverty or to resolve the problems of the women and children who come under their jurisdiction. The programs ameliorate some of the most pressing problems of the poor yet leave them in poverty with fundamental needs unmet. They may very well contribute to the breakup of families as well as discourage the formation of families.

In 1988 Congress passed the Family Security Act. This legislation amended the AFDC program in some significant ways. The new legislation will be phased in over a five-year period beginning in 1990. In chapter 6 we will examine this act and assess its impact on the nation's approach to welfare policy and the poor.

Chapter 5

Some Social Welfare Lessons from Europe

The major industrial countries of Western Europe have not eradicated poverty, but their poverty rates tend to be lower than the U.S. rate (Beckerman 1979; Commission of the European Communities 1981; OECD 1976). This is especially true of the Scandinavian countries, West Germany, Switzerland, and the Netherlands. The rate of poverty in France is similar to the U.S. rate, and Great Britain has a higher incidence of poverty (Townsend 1979).

The major Western countries are also experiencing increases in the numbers of female-headed families, which tend to have low incomes (Commission of the European Communities 1982; Finer et al. 1974; Kahn 1983). But almost all of these countries have comprehensive social welfare programs that provide more assistance and security for low-income, poor, and single-parent families than similar groups receive in the United States. Some of the countries do a much better job than the United States of assisting lone-parent families with children and aiding women, married and unmarried, who combine work with parenting. The programs of these countries are the focus of this chapter.

Some Limits of Comparative Analysis

Comparative analysis can provide interesting and even important insights about both positive and negative approaches to social policy, but conclusions must be tempered by caution (Mahler and Katz 1988). Three points should be kept in mind when comparing the successes of various countries in preventing, alleviating, or eradicating poverty. First, social welfare programs are not the only predictors of rates of national poverty. Countries with very healthy economies (especially very low rates of unemployment) have less need for assistance programs. The size of the nation's population may also be a factor. Large industrial nations with more complex economic and social problems may employ imaginative and costly social welfare programs and economic strategies but still have serious problems with poverty. The smaller industrial countries—Switzerland, Austria, Sweden, and Denmark, for example—have healthier economies and less poverty than those with larger populations. These smaller countries may have more success, in part, because they have less complex problems.

Second, just because a particular program works well in one country does not mean that it could be adopted or would work as well in another. The national health insurance systems in most Western European countries, for example, were adopted before health-care professionals became well organized and politically powerful. Since the end of World War II medical associations in the United States have been powerful enough to defeat proposals for fundamental reform of the health-care system. It is doubtful that either the Democratic or the Republican party would seriously consider proposing the creation of a national health insurance program in the United States today.

Third, there is a critical difference between maintaining families at a low-income level and helping them achieve a normal standard of living. Great Britain is an example of a country that uses social welfare programs to maintain large numbers of families far below median family income levels for long periods of time. This approach keeps the families from suffering absolute deprivation, but it does not solve their problems (such as the need for a decent job). Because the productive value of the recipients is lost, this type of welfare system also creates a serious drag on the economy. Modeling reform on Great Britain's approach would be a serious mistake.

The West European Approach

America's approach to social welfare policy is fundamentally different from that of most other Western industrial countries (Furniss and Mitchell 1984). There are three major differences. First, most of the Western industrial countries emphasize prevention of social problems, including poverty, by means of such policies as national health systems, extensive housing programs, and child or family allowances. Second, there is a belief that problems are best prevented if the most important programs are universal. Thus, these countries are much less likely to use means tests for program eligibility. Universal programs are not only more effective in preventing social ills, they generally enjoy broader public support and do not carry the social stigma often associated with means-tested welfare programs. Third, many of the countries try to ameliorate social problems by public intervention to keep the economy healthy. The Scandinavian countries, for example, use public resources to keep the unemployment rate as low as possible. Low rates of unemployment play a significant role in alleviating poverty.

Comparing U.S. social welfare programs for low-income families with those of Western Europe reveals how significantly these differences manifest themselves in public policy. The United States is the only major Western industrial country that (DeSario 1989; Kahn 1983; Kamerman 1980):

• does not have a uniform cash-benefit program for poor families;

• restricts cash-welfare benefits almost exclusively to single-parent families headed by women;

- has designed its main cash-welfare program to discourage mothers from working;
- has no statutory maternity benefits;
- has no universal child-rearing benefits; and
- has no universal health-care benefits (Kamerman 1984).

Some of the implications of these differences are fairly obvious. In the United States:

- The emphasis is on dealing with families or individuals after they become poor or seriously ill.
- Assistance is designed to be temporary, varies significantly by state, and is limited mostly to families headed by single women who must remain single to receive help.
- Little or nothing is done to move most welfare mothers into the job market, and in fact most are discouraged from seeking work by loss of benefits and lack of supportive services (e.g., child care).
- Poor families can receive critical assistance (e.g., medical care) only if they stay on welfare.
- Most employed women cannot have a child without suffering serious wage loss, or even loss of their job.

Social welfare programs in most of the European nations have been under stress during the last few years. These nations are suffering very low birth rates, aging populations, an increase in early retirements, and high rates of unemployment (Brookes 1988; Bureau of the Census 1988b; Haanes-Olsen 1989; OECD 1988; Social Security Administration 1988). The nations vary in their attempts to cope with these problems, but none has abandoned a strong commitment to social welfare. Primarily the nations are trying to stimulate private pension programs to supplement public retirement programs, encouraging personal savings, increasing the cost sharing for medical programs, extending retirement age, and encouraging employment, especially for young adults. To promote childbearing and employment of both parents, family allowances, parental leaves, and child care benefits have been increased in many of the nations (Haanes-Olsen 1989; Lindbeck 1988). The remainder of this chapter examines the major European programs and discusses the insights that might be applied in reforming American social welfare policies.

Child and Family Allowances

Every Western industrialized country except the United States provides a package of cash and in-kind programs to supplement the income of families with children (Kahn 1983; Kamerman 1980; Kamerman and Kahn 1981). Many countries call this set of programs a "family benefit" package. A central component is the child or family allowance, which can be found in sixty-seven countries (Haanes-Olsen 1989, 20; Kamerman 1984, 263). In most of them, including Canada, Belgium, and the Scandinavian countries, the allowances are universal and tax-free to all families, regardless of income or family structure. In some countries they are limited to families with two or more children, and sometimes they are means-tested. The allowances vary by the number of children in the family, and sometimes by the age of the children. France, for example, provides a larger supplement to families with young children. In all the major Western countries a special supplement is provided to single-parent families. None of the countries excludes families from these benefits because they are intact or because a parent is in the labor force.

The allowances were originally designed to increase the birth rate. Whether the grants ever had a significant impact on childbearing is problematical, but they remain popular because they supplement the cost of raising children. By sharing the cost of child rearing, the society helps insure that the basic needs of children are met. The general belief is that children raised in a more financially sound environment will be healthier, better educated, and more productive members of society.

The size of the grants is generally small, but the evidence suggests that they are a significant aid to low-income—especially single-parent—families (Kamerman 1984, 263). This is especially true since the allowance is larger when there is a lone parent.

Housing Assistance and Allowances

Governments in Western Europe use a wide range of policies to subsidize the construction, purchase, and rental of quality housing. Their role in housing tends to be substantially greater than that of the U.S. government (Hallett 1988; Headey 1978; Leichter and Rodgers 1984; McGuire 1981). Many of the West European governments became involved in housing policy in an effort to overcome the destruction brought about by two world wars. Once involved, they tended to stay involved. Both conservative and liberal political parties in Western Europe generally support an extensive role for the government in housing. The conservatives believe that government programs subsidize and stimulate the private housing market and the economy, while liberal parties add that decent housing for all should be a societal goal. Quality housing is a national resource because it is a durable good which also provides a healthier environment for families.

The governments of Western Europe use a wide range of housing policies, including public housing, saving bonuses to help families accumulate the down payment for a home, subsidies to builders or nonprofit housing cooperatives, assistance to home mortgage lenders, and housing allowances. Great Britain, for example, stresses public housing and housing allowances. About 20 percent of all housing in Britain is publicly owned. A wide range of income groups live in this public housing, with rents reflecting the size and income of the family. Housing allowances are also used to assist families living in privately owned housing.

In Sweden some 45 percent of all housing was built with public funds, about 20 percent is owned by consumer cooperatives, and about 35 percent is privately owned. Regardless of sector, about 90 percent of all housing in Sweden is financed by the government. This policy lowers the costs of housing, making it generally more affordable. In addition, Sweden has a very generous housing allowance policy. About 50 percent of all families with children are eligible for a housing allowance.

The governments of France, West Germany, and the Netherlands all play a major role in housing. Like Sweden, these countries stimulate the housing market through quasi-public housing subsidized and financed by the government and run by quasi-public authorities. Public and quasi-public housing is not limited to low-income families in these countries; it is commonly occupied by middle-income families. This takes away any stigma on public housing and promotes a healthier housing environment. These countries also use housing allowances to assist families with limited incomes. West Germany and France provide larger grants to single-parent families; the Netherlands and Great Britain increase the grants to families whose rent is high in relationship to their income.

Single-parent families benefit greatly from the housing programs in all these countries. They are given preference in public or quasi-public housing and receive housing allowances. In some countries they receive a larger allowance to make up for the loss or lack of a second adult earner. In most of these countries the housing allowance, along with the family or child allowance, constitutes a significant income grant to single-parent families. As Kamerman (1984 264–265) notes:

> If one adds the value of the housing allowance to the family allowance allotted a non-wage-earning mother the total accounts for almost half of her income in France, more than a third in Sweden, and more than a quarter in Germany and the United Kingdom; for the working mother, the transfers together constitute almost 40 percent of her income in France, more than 25 percent in Sweden, and close to that in the United Kingdom and Germany.

One obvious result of the use of family and housing allowances is that single-parent and other low-income families are much less dependent upon cash means-tested welfare programs.

Child Support

In recent years some countries have adopted a new approach to child support when one parent is absent. Austria, France, Denmark, and Sweden, among others, now use "advance maintenance payments" (Kahn 1988; Kamerman 1988; Kamerman and Kahn 1983). Under this program, all absent parents are taxed a certain proportion of their income each month. The proceeds are accumulated and used to provide a minimum monthly grant to all children with an absent parent. If the absent parent is unemployed or cannot be found or identified, the child or children still receive the minimum grant. An absent parent may also make additional contributions directly to the children.

The advance maintenance payments program enjoys growing popularity. One attraction of the policy is that it increases the chance that an absent parent will make regular payments. The program does so not by penalizing the parent, but by assessing the absent parent at a fair and regular rate. The burden on the absent parent is often reduced by the monthly tax which keeps the parent from falling behind and then being obligated to pay a sizable amount to catch up. Additionally, children are not penalized if the absent parent cannot pay or cannot be located. Last, requiring absent parents to meet their child-care obligations reduces the likelihood that the custodial parent and children will need public assistance.

The advance maintenance approach may work better in the four West European countries than it would in the United States. The reason, as noted above, is that many of the European social welfare programs that support and assist low-income families are universal, with no means tests. By contrast, a single-parent family in the United States often becomes ineligible for health or nutritional assistance when income from a job or child support increases, even very modestly (Kamerman 1989).

Maternity Benefits

Most of the major West European industrial countries have programs that protect the jobs and incomes of women for a period of time before and after childbirth (Kahn 1983; Kamerman 1980). Maternity leaves are generally covered by the country's social insurance program. This approach assures that a woman will receive the assistance regardless of the wealth of her employer. There is no means test for the program, benefits are in cash, and they are usually wage-related. In most cases a woman receives at least 90 percent of her normal wage up to some cutoff point. The leave lasts sixteen weeks in France and thirty-six weeks in Sweden, but most countries set the leave at twenty-four to twenty-six weeks, allowing for extensions for specified periods if the mother or child is ill (Kamerman and Kahn 1981, 71–73). Some countries allow a mother to extend the leave for a few weeks at her discretion, but at a reduced benefit level. Sweden allows the parents to decide, after the birth of the child, which of them will take the leave.

The social insurance programs also usually allow a mother to take a paid leave to care at home for a sick child. The mother usually receives 90 percent of her normal pay for a certain number of days. If the child's illness is extended, the mother is sometimes covered at the rate specified for personal illness under the social insurance program. Sweden allows either parent to take this leave.

Child Care

The issue of child care provides interesting insights into social welfare philosophy (Kahn 1987). In many of the Western European countries, as in the United States, there has been intense debate about the role that public authorities should play in child care. The family policies or family benefit packages that exist in Western Europe were built on the assumption that most mothers would remain at home until their children reached school age. As women have become more career-oriented and have formed a larger percentage of the work force, child-care policy has had to be reexamined. A few countries, especially in Scandinavia, have in recent years concluded that women should be given the support they need to be mothers and career employees at the same time (Kamerman 1988; Kamerman and Kahn 1981; Rosengren 1973; Wagner and Wagner 1976; Young and Nelson 1973). This decision reflects the existence of both a more liberal social philosophy and a labor shortage in these countries.

By contrast, other European countries have traditionally encouraged mothers to stay at home with their children until they are enrolled in preschool (around age three). In recent years some countries have accepted the change in women's roles and have begun to develop policies designed to accommodate mothers who want to return to the job market before their children enter preschool or who need child care during non-school hours. Some countries have established publicly supported or subsidized child-care centers, with fees scaled to income. Only France has created enough facilities to match demand to any significant degree. In West Germany and Great Britain there are long waiting lists for the facilities that have been established and there is continued reluctance about facilitating the return to the job market of women with small children. In most of the countries the mothers must pay for family or center care.

In Scandinavia the governments tend to play a much larger role in providing child care, but facilities are still inadequate to meet demand. The publicly supported centers in Sweden, for example, have long waiting lists. Still, the obligation of providing child-care assistance has been accepted and the facilities are being expanded. In Sweden the public centers are neighborhood-based and run by certified child-care specialists. A board composed of center employees and parents sets broad policy and supervises the operation of the center. Fees reflect the salary of the parent, the number of children in the family, and how long the center cares for the child each day. Fees are kept modest to encourage center use, and they are lower for single-parent families. All of the centers have a developmental, as opposed to custodial, orientation. Each child receives educational, nutritional, and health-care assistance. Some centers are open twenty-four hours a day for parents who work nights. Often the centers share facilities with programs for retired citizens who can, if they wish, help out with the children.

In sum, it is in child-care policy that other Western industrial countries most resemble the United States. Although in France and in Scandinavia there has been acceptance of the need for a larger public role in child care, in none of the countries is the demand for child-care assistance currently being met.

Health Care

Most advanced industrial countries in the West—except the United States—have a universal program of national health insurance or a national health service (Cairncross 1988; Leichter 1979; Navarro 1989; Roemer 1977; Simanis and Coleman 1980; Social Security Administration, 1988). These programs provide comprehensive health care to all citizens regardless of income, age, family structure, or employment status. While all individuals and families have the same benefits under the programs, low-income citizens and families certainly receive a higher level of health assistance than they would if care were based on ability to pay. Additionally, a family struggling on limited income cannot be made poorer by health-care costs, nor does the family have to be officially designated as poor—and then stay poor—in order to receive health-care assistance. Thus, the health-care system is one method by which these countries prevent poverty.

All the countries place emphasis on preventive health care, which is considered less costly than an acute health-care approach where people seek medical care only after they become ill. In a preventive system, emphasis is placed on health education and on such services as basic medical screening for early detection of conditions that can cause serious illness, maternity care, and prenatal and postnatal care. Most of the countries have networks of neighborhood centers that specialize in maternity and child health care. In France, mothers cannot receive their child or family allowance unless they schedule regular visits to these clinics for themselves and their children.

With the exception of Great Britain, all the major Western European industrial countries have national health insurance systems. Under these systems, most citizens become a member of the national health insurance program through their employment. All employers are obligated to enroll their employees in an approved insurance plan that provides comprehensive health-care coverage to the employee and any dependents. Both the employer and the employee pay a monthly fee, which provides most of the funding for the system. Any citizen who is unemployed or aged is enrolled in a health plan financed by the federal and/or local government.

Under national health insurance, participants select a doctor of their choice, who either treats them or, if necessary, refers them to a specialist. The doctors charge on a fee-for-service basis, but the government establishes the reimbursement rate. The patient may pay a small fee for services, especially if medical appliances or drugs are prescribed.

Germany was the first Western country to adopt a health insurance program, the Sickness Insurance Law of 1883 (Flora and Heidenheimer 1981; Sulzbach 1947). Originally the act covered industrial wage earners but not their families. In 1885 and 1886 the law was amended to bring some workers in commercial enterprises and farm work into the program. The program, financed by a tax on workers and their employers, provided medical care, cash sickness benefits, maternity benefits, and a cash grant for funeral expenses. The program was administered by sickness funds, a type of cooperative organization that had long existed in Germany. In 1885 there were almost 19,000 such funds.

During the first two decades of the twentieth century, the program changed in two major ways. Eligibility was extended to more workers and increasingly to their dependents, and benefits became more comprehensive. National standards for the sickness funds encouraged them to consolidate, which greatly reduced their numbers. Hundreds of amendments strengthened and expanded the program over the years. Currently almost all West German citizens are covered by the program. Employees make monthly contributions, which are matched by employers. Some of the costs are financed out of general revenues. All citizens earning less than a regularly adjusted minimum income standard are required to participate in the program, and their dependents are automatically covered. Those earning above the standard may participate on a voluntary basis. Pensioners and citizens receiving unemployment compensation are covered by public programs.

Medical benefits under the German program are comprehensive, with modest cost sharing. In addition to comprehensive health care, the program provides sickness allowances, a household allowance so that families can hire assistance during an illness, a lump-sum maternity payment, and a cash grant to cover funeral expenses. Doctors are paid on a fee-for-service basis, with fee schedules determined by the federal government.

The national health insurance systems in other Western industrial countries work very much like the West German system. National health insurance is not inexpensive, but it provides comprehensive coverage for all citizens for about the same per capita cost as the American system (Haanes-Olsen 1989, 24; Simanis and Coleman 1980, 5).

Great Britain established a national insurance plan in 1911.The initial plan covered workers, but not their dependents. The 1911 act was designed to supplement and, in part, take the place of worker organizations known as friendly societies, cooperative organizations that pooled fees to provide workers with cash benefits during illness, medical care by a contracted physician, and an allowance to cover funeral expenses.

The 1911 act covered only workers earning less than an established income standard. The program was financed by worker and employer contributions and general tax revenues. Covered workers received physician care (but not hospitalization) and sickness, disability, and maternity benefits. The friendly societies were pacified by being allowed to administer all but the medical benefits. By the 1940s only about 40 percent of the population was covered under the act (Leichter 1979, 167).

To overcome many of the inadequacies of this approach, the National Health Service Act was passed in 1948. Under this act, the government assumed responsibility for financing hospital and clinic construction and for training and hiring medical personnel. Unlike a national health insurance system, the government became the owner of the country's hospitals and clinics and the employer of most doctors and other medical personnel. Some 85 percent of the cost of the program is financed by the central and local governments. Employers and employees pay modest insurance premiums that finance another 10 percent of costs. Cost-sharing and user fees provide the other 5 percent of financing.

Every British citizen is covered under the act, and the benefits are comprehensive. Citizens receive routine medical care by registering with a physician of their choice. General practitioners receive a fee for each patient registered with them. As a cost-cutting incentive, group practitioners are allowed to have more patients than solo practitioners. Hospital and surgical care is provided by physicians who are salaried employees of publicly owned hospitals. Patients pay a small fee for dental and ophthalmic services and for prescriptions. There are normally no fees associated with routine medical and hospital services.

The British Health Service has been plagued by a very weak national economy, preventing the nation from increasing funding to upgrade medical services. Still, the British National Health Service, like the health-care programs found in the other Western nations, provides comprehensive health care to all citizens, regardless of their income.

Market Strategies

Many Western industrial countries use economic strategies to reduce the need for social welfare assistance. One of the most common strategies is the use of economic policies and public programs to keep unemployment as low as possible. Norway and Sweden, for example, have been successful in keeping unemployment below 3 percent (Haanes-Olsen 1989, n16; Office of Economic Research 1981, 10). They do so through the manipulation of interest rates, public investments in the private sector, and government job training, relocation, and employment programs (Furniss and Tilton 1979, 134–38). By contrast, American administrations have often used economic policies to increase the unemployment rate as a method of reducing or controlling the rate of inflation.

Keeping unemployment low is often part of a more complex economic strategy. Sweden, for example, has made economic efficiency a key element in its market approach. The Swedes believe that their industry must be modern and highly productive in order to remain competitive in international markets. This means that industry must constantly innovate to promote productivity, and that weak, inefficient businesses must be weeded out. The maintenance of obsolete or inefficient jobs is not allowed because this would reduce efficiency. Workers and unions do not have to struggle to protect obsolete jobs, for workers whose jobs are abolished are assured of other, equally good positions. If the worker needs retraining or relocation, he or she receives this help with pay during the transition period. Thus, full employment is part of a larger economic strategy designed to keep the economy healthy, competitive, and prosperous. Sweden recognizes that only this type of economy can produce the surpluses needed to provide a wide range of supportive human services.

Summary and Conclusions

The social welfare systems of other major Western industrial societies differ from the American system in several important respects. First, most of these countries provide a broader core of universal, non-means-tested assistance programs to all citizens. The most obvious example is the package of programs provided to all citizens through the health-care system. Second, the countries have programs specifically designed to assist families with children. These programs are either universal or provided to almost all middle- and low-income families. All the countries make this package available to lone-parent families, with many giving such families a larger supplement. Third, none of them denies assistance to intact families or requires a lone parent to stay unemployed, single, or poor to qualify for, or remain qualified for, critical assistance such as housing or health care. Fourth, the cash-benefit programs are uniform for all poor families, regardless of family structure (Kamerman and Kahn 1988).

Because of the benefits that citizens receive from programs such as national health insurance, family allowances, varied housing programs, and maternity leaves, fewer low-income families need income-tested cash-welfare assistance. The universal and other broadly provided assistance programs thus increase the security, independence, and presumably the dignity of low-income families, allowing them more options for work, training, or education. France has specifically altered and expanded its social welfare package in recent years to give greater assistance to lone-parent families and to allow low-income women a choice of staying home with their children or entering the labor force. Sweden has designed its system to facilitate management of simultaneous work and parenting roles by both parents.

This review suggests that for several reasons the social welfare programs of Western Europe are better designed than the U.S. programs. First, they better meet many of the basic, critical needs of citizens. This is especially true of health-care and housing programs. The universal financing of such programs as health care and maternity leaves allows all citizens to enjoy these benefits regardless of the wealth of their employer. Second, they do not require a parent to be single or remain single or unemployed in order to receive needed assistance. These negative incentives are built into the American system. Third, they provide a uniform level of benefits to all poor families, including intact or single-parent families that fall on hard times. There are lessons here that could inform alterations in the American approach to social welfare.

Some West European programs are particularly imaginative and provide cues about how American programs could be improved.

Most obvious is the advance maintenance payments program now in effect in a number of countries. Sweden's universally financed maternity leave, which can be used by either parent, and the broadly available housing allowances found in West Germany, France, and Sweden are other good examples.

Last, the market strategy of some of these countries yields a critical insight. The health of a country's economy is the key predictor of the poverty rate. Public policies designed to keep unemployment low, productivity high, and industries competitive, and to support, retrain, and relocate those out of the job market are critical means by which a nation can limit poverty.

Chapter 6

Reforming the American Welfare System

Establishing, updating, or revising welfare programs has never been easy in the United States. As noted earlier, it took the crisis of the Great Depression and the turmoil of the 1960s to produce the patchwork system of programs that we currently refer to as the American welfare system. Richard Nixon tried diligently to reform the welfare system, hoping to substitute a version of the negative income tax* for most of the extant programs. His plan was twice passed by the House, but it died from lack of action by the Senate.

Although President Nixon's proposal finally failed, it promoted a consensus about the most plausible approach to welfare reform. Gerald Ford made a modest effort to recoup Nixon's momentum on the issue by offering another reform package based on the negative income tax. Ford abandoned the effort when the economy turned increasingly sour. Jimmy Carter hoped that welfare reform would be a major accomplishment of his administration. He proposed a system based on a negative income tax for those able to

---

*In the simplest terms, under a negative income tax system a family's (or individual's) income is compared to a predetermined poverty threshold. If a family's income is above the threshold, it will pay an income tax. If it is below the threshold, the family has a "negative income" and the government will transfer income to the family to bring it up to the poverty level.

work, and a guaranteed income for those who were unemployable. President Carter's plan also foundered in Congress.

The defeat of Carter's plan cast a pale over reform for most of a decade. The concepts on which that plan was based had been debated during three administrations, and it seemed clear that Congress was unlikely to accept reform based on substantial use of the negative income tax plan. The consensus upon which debate centered during three administrations had clearly dissolved (Ellwood 1989, 269)

A New Consensus—Supported Work

President Ronald Reagan's idea of reform consisted of three principles: (1) compulsory work programs for the poor; (2) reducing or abolishing as many welfare programs as possible; and (3) convincing the states to assume a larger share of the costs and administrative burdens of those programs that survived. Equally important, Reagan's tax reduction plan combined with massive defense expenditures created huge deficits, making it even less likely that Congress would entertain welfare reforms that would significantly raise federal outlays, even temporarily. Additionally, in the early and mid-1980s there was no generalized crisis of the magnitude that had spawned programs in the 1930s, 1940s, 1960s, or early 1970s. Poverty increased quite dramatically during the Reagan years, but Reagan was successful in dismissing this as a temporary aberration of his economic policies.

While Reagan's convictions never changed, by the end of his presidency a new consensus on welfare reform was developing in Congress and at the state level. The new consensus is that poverty alleviation can best be achieved by programs that broadly train welfare mothers for employment and then provide them with assistance to help them stay in the work force, and by the adoption of a series of nonwelfare programs designed to prevent poverty by strengthening families, improving human skills, and supporting employees (Cook 1989; Gutmann 1988; Weir, Orloff, and Skocpol 1988).

The first set of programs are currently referred to as workfare plans, supported work, or mutual obligation contracts. They differ substantially from programs that simply require some welfare recipients to work in return for benefits. These new training and work programs are backed by programs such as child care and medical benefits, helping the family head to stay in the work force. The second set of programs might be publicly or privately supported and are often thought of as nonwelfare options because they are funded by employers or provided to a wide range of families, including many who are above the poverty level.

Some of the supportive or nonwelfare policies currently under debate include an array of both publicly and privately supported child-care options. There is also increasing emphasis on improving child support enforcement, maternity leaves, enriched educational programs for all school children, tax reforms to benefit all low-income households, and sex education as a method of reducing the size and number of female-headed households. There are also proposals before Congress to improve the retirement benefits of women who move in and out of the job market (primarily because of family responsibilities), and women who choose to maintain a household. These and other nonwelfare options such as education and job training programs for youths will be discussed in more detail below, along with recent alterations of the AFDC program, improved housing programs, and better nutrition and health-care programs.

A combination of nonwelfare and reformed or modestly expanded welfare, education, and job training programs could form the core of an improved, if highly imperfect, antipoverty strategy in the United States. Ideally, social welfare programs should be designed to prevent social problems. Enlightened public policies in areas such as housing, employment, health care, education, and child support can promote this goal. Social welfare programs are also generally more effective if they are universal. Inclusive programs help prevent social problems, do not stigmatize recipients, and enjoy much broader public support. Programs based on social insurance are also more acceptable to the public because they are based on reciprocity, and they spread and share costs. Last, social welfare programs are more acceptable to the public if they supplement individual efforts to be self-supporting.

Realistically, poverty researchers tend to agree that because of budgetary restraints, welfare reforms in the near future are not likely to be substantial enough to meet these ideal standards. Nor are the reforms likely to significantly alter the lives of most welfare recipients or greatly reduce the number of poor (Cottingham and Ellwood 1989). Most of America's poor, in fact, consist of the working poor and, for the most part, they will not be affected by reforms of welfare programs (Danziger 1989). Nonwelfare programs are currently receiving a great deal of attention, but progress here will also be slow in both the public and private sectors. Until better nonwelfare programs are in place, the reforms of AFDC and other welfare programs discussed below will not be very productive. Additionally, some of the major causes of poverty—inadequate growth in the economy, unemployment and subemployment, deficient public schools—do not generally command sufficient attention from those policy makers concerned about poverty and welfare costs. Thus, some progress can be made in the immediate future, but major alterations in the number or conditions of the American poor are not very likely.

In analyzing policy options, the critical question that we will focus on is the extent to which a combination of nonwelfare, welfare, and educational reforms can address the causes of poverty among female-headed households. Chapter 3 identified a series of correlates of poverty that can be grouped under three categories: the increasing number of broken families, the income problems of female-headed families, and the high unemployment rate of men, especially black men. Potential reforms are analyzed below, and the extent to which they would address the major causes of poverty among female-headed families is assessed.

Nonwelfare Options

There are many non-means-tested programs that could have an impact on the economic conditions of families, including those headed by women. These policies would also promote the family by removing some of the major economic strains that prevent the formation of families or contribute to their breakup. The most promising nonwelfare options may be discussed under three major categories: family policies, educational programs, and job programs.

Family Policies

Child or Family Allowances

Scholars who study social welfare programs often argue that the United States should adopt a universal family or child allowance program fashioned after those found in other Western industrialized nations (Kamerman 1984, 270). Even some conservatives (Gilder 1981, 153) have written in support of such an option. Proponents argue that the empirical evidence shows that the allowances promote family life by giving parents more financial security, which in turn creates a healthier, more stable environment for children. In the long run, proponents argue, improved family life promotes a better, more prosperous society that is less dependent upon public support.

The evidence presented in chapter 5 strongly supports this conclusion. Yet Congress has never given serious consideration to a universal child or family allowance. In large part, this lack of serious attention results from the categorical orientation of welfare programs in the United States. American policy makers are generally disinclined to consider programs that would aid all parents or children without regard to economic need. The kind of means-tested child allowance program found in nations such as West Germany might have more appeal. This type of program, however, could be established most easily through reform of the AFDC program or the Earned Income Tax Credit (Lerman 1989).

The Earned Income Tax Credit

The United States does have a version of a family allowance, which with some revisions could approximate the programs found in

Europe. The Earned Income Tax Credit (EITC) was added to the Internal Revenue Code in 1975. The EITC provides an annual earning supplement to parents who maintain a household for a child, have modest earnings and taxable income. The EITC is the only tax credit that is refundable. If the parents do not owe any taxes or have a tax obligation lower than the credit, they receive a direct payment from the Internal Revenue Service. This program was adopted to give low-income parents a "work bonus" or incentive to work, and to compensate for the regressive impact of the Social Security tax.

In 1989 the credit equaled 14 percent of the first $5,714 of earnings, or a maximum of $800. Between $9,000 and $17,000 the credit phases out. The base is automatically adjusted each year to reflect inflation.

The EITC gives low-income families with dependent children some financial assistance, but it is flawed in major ways. First, a low-income parent does not qualify for the credit unless he or she earns enough income to provide at least 50 percent of the support of the children in the family. A single mother receiving 50 percent or more of her income from AFDC would not qualify for the credit. Second, the credit does not vary by number of children in the family. Third, even those families that qualify for the credit receive it only at the end of the year in a lump sum.

The EITC could be amended in any number of ways to create a family or child allowance program that could provide much better assistance to low-income parents. Most obviously, the credit could be raised, a larger proportion of income from welfare programs could be counted, the credit could be estimated and paid out monthly to low-income families, and benefits could vary by family size.

Every year during the 1980s Congress has debated many potential reforms of this program. Since it is already on the books, and because there are many options for making it a better program, it provides Congress with a viable method of improving the conditions of low-income parents, including single mothers.

Child Support

As shown in chapter 3, a significant percentage of all mothers, including a majority of minority women, are not awarded child support in divorce or separation agreements. Those who are awarded support generally receive low allotments, and most get only part of the support they have been awarded. Many divorced and separated women and their dependents live in, or close to, poverty because they receive inadequate or no support from the absent parent. The number of children affected by child support is enormous. One researcher has estimated that half of all children will become eligible for child support before reaching the age of eighteen (Bumpass 1984).

Two reforms could improve this situation. First, the states could do a better job of requiring identification of the absent parent, seeing that reasonable support is awarded, and enforcing the requirement that the support be paid. One major reason why absent parents stop making payments is that once they fall behind, the sum owed grows and they become discouraged about ever being able to make the debt good. States can deal with this problem in part by carefully monitoring payments and using garnishment of wages to keep payments current and the size of the debt in check. Congress has recently passed legislation to improve state efforts (Garfinkel, McLanahan, and Wong 1988, 70–71). The recent reforms of AFDC, discussed below, address another part of this problem. One researcher has estimated that if all fathers of children on AFDC were identified, assessed 25 percent of their salary in support, and made to pay that support, the average AFDC mother would receive $3,000 a year. In 1984 the average AFDC mother actually received only $225. Thus, better enforcement would reduce AFDC costs quite substantially (Lerman 1989, 234).

The second reform is more substantial and would draw upon the Swedish advance maintenance plan discussed in chapter 5. An American version of the plan has been suggested by Garfinkel and associates (Garfinkel, McLanahan, and Wong 1988; Garfinkel and Uhr 1984). First, all noncustodial parents would be subject to a child support tax. This tax would be withheld from the parent's pay, much like the Social Security contribution. The tax would vary according to the number of children. For example, the tax on the first $60,000 in earnings might be 17 percent for one child, 25 percent for two children, increasing to a maximum of 33 percent for six or more. Second, all children with an absent parent would receive a monthly benefit equal to the tax or a minimum, whichever is higher.

The advantages of this plan are obvious. First, all children with an absent parent would receive support—either from the parent or from federal revenues. Second, all children would receive a minimum benefit. Thus, children of a poor or unemployed parent would still receive assistance. Third, since the tax is deducted from each paycheck, the absent parent cannot fall behind. This is not only more efficient, it requires all parents to face the fact that they will always have a financial responsibility for their children. Last, the program would probably lower the poverty rate for female household heads and their dependents. Even if the impact on poverty were not major, such a program would lower the costs of AFDC.

A demonstration project is currently being conducted in Wisconsin to determine if the plan would lower the poverty and dependency rate and produce a net saving. Several years into the project, the outcomes have been quite positive (Garfinkel and Uhr 1984, 120). A simulation of the implications of implementing this program nationwide produced very interesting insights. The researchers generated three models based on varying levels of success in collecting from absent parents and various levels of guaranteed benefits. They found that at 70 percent, 80 percent, or 100 percent effectiveness, the program would reduce the poverty gap for poor families between 38 and 53 percent, and that AFDC caseloads would decrease by 48 to 64 percent. At 100 percent collection effectiveness, the program would generally produce a saving, with the cost rising above current levels as collection effectiveness falls and benefit levels increase (Garfinkel, McLanahan and Wong 1988, 80). These findings strongly suggest the value of improving child support across the nation.

Child Care

One of the most critical needs of parents who want or need to be employed or to enter educational or job training programs is adequate, affordable child care (Beyna, Bell, and Trutko 1984; Dubnoff 1986; Polit and O'Hara 1989; Scoll and Engstrom 1985; SCCYF 1987a). The demand for child care is currently very high and can be expected to increase in the future. The population of children under six will grow from 19.6 million in 1980 to an estimated 22.9 million in 1990. The number of children under ten in single-parent households is also expected to increase, from 6 to 9 million, during this period. And, of course, both married and unmarried women are increasing their participation in the work force. Currently over half of all single and married mothers with young children are employed, although most are not employed full time, year round. By the year 2000 some 75 percent of all mothers will be employed outside the home (Kamerman and Kahn 1987).

According to a study by the Bureau of the Census (1982a, 15–19), many mothers report that they would enter the job market if child care were available. This includes 26 percent of all mothers not in the job market. The figure increases to 36 percent of women in a household with an annual income below $15,000, and 45 percent of single mothers. Additionally, 21 percent of all mothers working part time said that they would increase their work hours if they could obtain child care.

Any reform effort would have to deal with four separate child-care problems: inadequate supply, lack of knowledge about options, quality control, and cost barriers. In some parts of the country, day-care centers have six- to twelve-month waiting lists. Also, low-income mothers often are uninformed about publicly or privately financed child-care options. Cost is a major problem for many families. Studies indicate that care for one child ranges from

$2,500 to $6,500 a year, with the average cost being about $3,000. Obviously, these costs are prohibitive for many families, especially those headed by a lone parent.

Quality control is a very difficult problem because child care is so diversely provided. A majority of children in child care are in care outside their homes, with the largest percentage being in family day-care facilities. In 1985 a congressional committee estimated that 70 to 90 percent of these facilities are unlicensed (SCCYF 1985). A number of national surveys of day care facilities have concluded that the quality of care provided by both family and center day care is generally of average to low quality (Clarke-Stewart 1982; Fosburg and Hawkins 1981; Keyserling 1972).

The problems may be even worse where infant care is concerned. A recent study (Young and Zigler 1986) found that forty-seven states do not meet minimal standards for staffing day-care centers for infants. The three major problems the study uncovered were: little if any training for workers, minimal qualifications for staff, and high ratios of infants to adults. This study was restricted to licensed day-care centers. Most infants, however, are cared for in unlicensed homes and centers. The authors of this study point out (p. 52) that conditions in unlicensed facilities are most likely even worse.

The federal role

Child care is such a massive problem that its solution must be a combined private, corporate, and government effort. States must bear the major public responsibility, just as they do in education. The federal government does, however, have a critical role. In designing any solution it is inescapable that the federal government will have to increase significantly its commitment to child care. The major direct federal program that supports child care is the Social Services Block Grant, generally referred to as Title XX. Until 1981, Title XX required states to set aside $200 million of all Title XX funds for child care. In fact, the states spent about 18 percent of all Title XX funds on child care, totaling about $720 million in 1980. In 1981 Congress cut funding for Title XX by 20 percent, and the states were given the option of deciding how much they wanted to spend on child care. Since 1981 the states have spent less on child care, but Title XX still provides the largest direct federal support for these services. About $388 million went to child care in 1986, although state spending varies considerably (Robins 1988, 4). In inflation-adjusted dollars, twenty-nine states spent less for child care funded through Title XX in 1986 than in 1981 (Blank and Wilkins 1986, 4).

The states are spending less because they are receiving less and because the set-aside was eliminated. An obvious option would be to expand funding for the Social Services Block Grant and require the states to use the new funds for child-care services. The states could use these funds in a variety of ways. For example, the states might use some of the funds to subsidize providers of child-care services to low-income families. The states would have the option of providing more lucrative incentives to public or private agencies offering child-care services to specific low-income parents, such as single parents. To make certain that these services were afford-able for low-income parents, day-care providers receiving subsi-dies could be required to use sliding-fee scales. Some of the money might be used to match state expenditures on full-day kindergartens in public schools. States might also qualify for matching funds to improve child-care monitoring systems. The states would also have the option of providing subsidies and technical assistance to part-nerships between public and private organizations committed to providing more child care for low-income families.

Another option would be for the states to fund startup costs for umbrella organizations that would provide training and certifica-tion to providers of family day-care services. The umbrella orga-nization ideally would also monitor family day care, provide financial assistance, and develop methods of sharing resources. The providers of family day care can be given many incentives to cooperate with the umbrella organization, including certification for participation in the Child Care Food Program. Participation in these programs ensures that the nutritional and health needs of the children receive some attention.

Young and Zigler (1986) recommend three additional methods by which the federal government could play a role in improving the quality of day care. First, they propose establishment of a national day-care clearing house within the federal bureaucracy. The clearing house would provide public officials, parents, and care providers with the latest and best information available on the characteristics, impact, and operation of quality day care. Second, they recommend developing a model for day-care programs based on Head Start, which emphasizes an educational partnership between parents and providers. A central component of these model programs would be a parental right to unlimited access to their child's program, and a responsibility on the part of the provider to furnish parents with periodic progress reports (Young and Zigler 1986, 53).

A third suggestion is that public schools provide child care for three- to twelve-year-olds. During the school year the schools would provide care before and after school and full time during vacations. The authors recommend that the public schools provide a family support system for first-time parents, information and referral services, and support services for private day-care homes where most children under three are served. This policy approach would significantly alter the state's role in the provision of day care and would provide the greatest potential for expanding day-care services to all families in need.

The child-care tax credit

Another very important method by which the federal government could increase the availability and affordability of child care is by changes in the dependent-care tax credit. As currently written, this program provides little assistance to low-income families. Working parents who pay for child care receive a nonrefundable tax credit for each child. For example, for one child the credit applies to the first $2,400 of costs, and for two children it increases to $4,800. The credit decreases with income, with a minimum of 20 percent of outlays for families with a gross income above $28,000. Most families using the tax credit have incomes over $25,000; only 6 percent of all families using the credit in 1982 had incomes below $10,000 (Ways and Means 1985, 374). Low-income families receive little benefit from the credit because they generally do not have enough federal tax liability to use this option.

This program could be altered to increase child-care options for most families. The credit limits could be raised to reduce child-care expenses for most working families. As currently written the program provides modest assistance. In 1985 the average credit per family was $371 (Robins 1988, 5). Second, the program could be altered to give larger credits to low-income parents. Last, the credit could be made refundable so that low-income families would receive the full value of the deduction. This last option would provide more assistance to low-income families than to the severely poor if the credit would not be received until the end of the year. The poorest of families generally cannot benefit from tax credits because they have no way to meet out-of-pocket expenses, even if they might be reimbursed.

Latchkey children

Another issue that has to be faced is the growing problem of latchkey children. A latchkey child is one who is left unattended before or after school or during holidays because the parent or parents are at work. Estimates of the number of latchkey children vary from 2 to 7 million (SCCYF 1984c, 24). Some states use Title XX funds to finance care for latchkey children, but most Title XX funding is reserved for preschool programs. A recent study by the Children's Defense Fund reported that there were publicly or privately supported programs in about half the states (Blank and Wilkins 1986, 49–54). Often the public schools and community groups form a partnership to provide care for children after regular school hours or during holidays. Volunteer and charitable groups often provide "warm" phone lines that latchkey children can call to help them deal with fear, loneliness, or emergencies. Most of the states with programs meet the needs of only a small proportion of the children in need of care and often exclude poor families by cost barriers. The programs should be expanded considerably, and they need to be based on a sliding-fee schedule, with exemption from fees for the poorest families.

Zigler's recommendation above that the public schools play a major role in day care is particularly relevant for the latchkey problem. This option would accommodate the largest number of children and offers one additional advantage. Before-and-after-school care can do more than provide children with supervision and companionship. Studies reveal that children attending these programs show marked academic improvements and increased self-esteem (SCCYF 1984c, 30).

Preschool programs

One trend that might decrease the need for child care while assisting low-income families is the growing popularity of preschool programs for three- to five-year-olds. By 1982 over 36 percent of all three- and four-year-old children were in preschool, up from 20.5 percent in 1970. In 1985, 94 percent of five-year-olds attended kindergarten, up from 80 percent in 1970 and 71 percent in 1965. The popularity of pre-kindergarten and kindergarten programs reflects a growing appreciation of the educational advantages of earlier education. Growing evidence supports the conclusion that early education has long-term educational benefits, especially among disadvantaged students (Consortium for Longitudinal Studies 1978; Schweinhart and Weikart 1980).

The House Select Committee on Children, Youth and Families recently recommended that Congress pass legislation providing incentive grants to public and private nonprofit agencies to assist in establishing educational programs in the public schools for four-year olds. The committee recommended that special grants be established for districts that set up enrichment programs for disadvantaged children. The programs, the Committee concluded, should be based on sliding fees so that families from all income levels can participate (SCCYF 1984c, 18).

The private sector role

A positive trend in child care is that more corporations are getting involved. The most recent figures (Friedman 1986) indicate that about 3,000 corporations are providing child-care assistance of some type to their employees. As recently as 1978 only 110 corporations had child-care programs. While corporations are showing more awareness about the child-care needs of their employees, a great deal remains to be done. In 1986 there were approximately 44,000 corporations with 100 or more employees.

Corporations are increasingly involved in child care because a very large percentage of their employees are women with children, or fathers whose wives are also employed. Sixty percent of all married men now have a working wife, and presumably a more stressful home life. Studies conducted by or for corporations indicate that child-care services reduce employee stress, improve employee morale, lower absenteeism, and increase the recruitment advantage of the company (Burud, Aschbacher, and McCoskey 1984; Magid 1983; Perry 1982). The studies tend to be more impressionistic than rigorous, but the findings seem credible (Miller 1984).

The assistance being provided by corporations takes a number of forms, including child-care information and referral services, grants to state agencies involved in training and certifying child-care providers, voucher and cash-grant benefits to employees that can be used to pay for child care, company contracts with centers to obtain discounts for employees, and on-site child-care centers financed by corporations.

About 150 corporations have established on-site child-care centers for employees. Employees usually pay for this child care on a sliding-fee basis. Some corporations have individually or jointly elected to support and subsidize one or more centers for their employees. Other companies have helped organize and train personnel to run home or family day-care centers. Businesses have also collaborated with school districts and community agencies to run before- and after-school programs in schools, churches, and storefronts. A few companies have established summer day programs on or near company property. To deal with absenteeism, a number of companies provide nurses to stay with sick children or subsidize centers that specialize in looking after children who are ill.

One common form of corporate child care is information. Corporations either gather information on child-care facilities or they hire agencies that specialize in this service to assist their employees. IBM, for example, established a national contractor called Work/Family Directions to identify referral services and providers for employees in its 200 offices across the country.

As one option to help parents deal with the costs of day care, many corporations now offer their employees flexible benefits. The employee is offered a choice of benefits, one of which is a child-care subsidy. One option is encouraged by the tax code and is the fastest growing form of federal child-care assistance. The employee can opt to have the employer reduce his or her income by an agreed-upon amount. The employer pays the employee's child-care costs directly from this fund. The value to the employee is that his or her taxable income is reduced. As long as the value of the assistance is less than $5,000, it is a nontaxable benefit. Because of the tax rate, this option is of little benefit to families that earn less than $20,000 a year. For higher-income families, however, it will provide substantial assistance.

Some corporations are also introducing job sharing, flexitime, part-time work, and personal or sick child leave to reduce employees' needs for child care.

Act for Better Child-Care Services

In July 1989 the United States Senate passed the Act for Better Child-Care Services. This bill provides $1.75 billion a year to the states to subsidize child-care providers and make the dependent-care tax credit largely refundable, thereby expanding its availability to low-income parents who owe no taxes. The bill would also require the states to set standards for day-care providers. To encourage retirees to work in day-care centers, the bill relaxes the Social Security earning test and exempts child-care workers from it. The bill also provides a tax credit of up to $500 for one child and a maximum of $750 for two or more children to help cover the cost of health-insurance coverage (Hertzke and Scribner 1989). It is not clear whether this bill will be supported by the House or signed by the president.

Maternity Leaves

As noted in chapter 5, the United States is the only major industrial nation without a national policy covering maternity leaves. In most other Western industrial nations women who give birth are given an employment leave with assurance of job protection and retention of seniority and pension entitlements. In these nations the social security or social insurance system provides the new mother with a cash grant equal to all or part of the wage that she would have received from employment. In most countries the benefit level is 90 to 100 percent of the maximum wage covered by social insurance. Generally, the benefit is tax free and available to all women who have been employed for some minimum period before childbirth, regardless of income. Sweden, Norway, and Finland have expanded benefits to cover both parents, making them the only countries with genuine parental-leave policies.

All of the countries that provide maternity leaves also assume responsibility for medical and hospital coverage at birth, plus prenatal and postnatal care. Almost all the countries provide one-time benefits such as a small cash grant for infant clothing and furniture. The cash or in-kind grants are often contingent on the mother having one or more prenatal examinations.

As maternity policies have evolved and expanded to meet the

needs of working couples, many nations have added optional supplemental leaves for mothers who want to remain at home with their children for longer periods. These leaves start after regular maternity benefits are exhausted and usually provide a flat grant under the unemployment insurance system or under sickness insurance. These leaves are usually for a year or until the youngest child is two. Many countries allow a mother to opt for a longer, unpaid but job-protected leave if she wants to stay home with her young children.

The Pregnancy Discrimination Act of 1978 requires U.S. employers to treat pregnancy like any other disability or illness. In practice, this means that company insurance must cover the same share of costs that would normally be paid for an illness, and that the employer must give the mothers a short disability leave. The law does not require the employer to extend the leave beyond the immediate recovery period, or to guarantee the job security of the mother if she opts for a leave beyond the immediate recovery period.

In January 1987, in its first major interpretation of the Pregnancy Discrimination Act, the Supreme Court (*California Federal Savings and Loan Association v. Mark Guerra*, 93 L. Ed. 2d 613) upheld a state law that requires employers to grant special job protection to employees who are physically unable to work because of pregnancy. In a 6–3 decision the court upheld a California statute that requires employers to grant an unpaid leave of up to four months to women disabled by pregnancy or childbirth, even if similar leaves are not granted for other disabilities. The majority on the court argued that the Pregnancy Discrimination Act established a floor of benefits for pregnant women, not a ceiling. Justice Thurgood Marshall in the majority decision said: "By taking pregnancy into account, California's pregnancy leave statute allows women, as well as men, to have families without losing their jobs."

The Supreme Court's decision is a major victory for women, but the California law does not establish a universal maternity policy. It is, in fact, quite restrictive. It limits leaves to women physically disabled by pregnancy, childbirth, or related medical conditions. The full four months of leave would not be given unless there were special medical problems. The employer is obligated to give a woman back her job or an equivalent position, but only if economic conditions make this possible.

The states of Hawaii, New Jersey, New York, and Rhode Island have passed laws that are comparable to the California statute. The court's decision will undoubtedly stimulate other states to pass similar legislation. It will also provide ammunition to those members of Congress who have been trying to pass legislation establishing a national maternity policy. The author of one proposal, Pat Schroeder (D. Colorado), reacted to the opinion by saying: "The California decision has opened the doors for us. It says the Supreme Court recognizes there are women in the work force who are there to stay and that the demands of family have to be addressed by society" (*New York Times* 1987, 10).

Only a week after the California case, the Supreme Court ruled (*Wimberly v. Labor and Industrial Relations Commission*, 93 L. Ed. 2d 909) that a 1976 federal unemployment-compensation law prohibited discrimination against pregnant women, but did not require preferential treatment. In this case a woman took a leave to have a child without guarantee of reinstatement. Within a few weeks of having the child, she informed her employer that she would like to return to work. Upon being informed that no job was available, she applied for unemployment compensation. The state of Missouri refused her request under a neutral statute that denies unemployment compensation to any worker who leaves a job voluntarily.

The court's support of the Missouri law is in one sense of limited importance. Only three other states have unemployment-compensation laws as restrictive as Missouri's. The importance of the case, however, is that it clarifies the court's view that while Congress has prohibited discrimination against pregnant women, it has neither required that they be given preferential treatment nor prohibited preferential treatment.

It is unlikely that the maternity issue will be resolved very well in the United States unless the cost is spread among employers. Only the larger corporations are likely to accept the costs of paid leaves, and in fact many small employers probably could not afford to give their employees paid maternity leaves. Currently only about half of all women in the work force have some type of maternity benefit. Many of the nation's largest corporations provide a twelve- to sixteen-week leave to new mothers; most of these guarantee job protection. Some of these corporations also allow leaves for fathers, although corporate norms are not supportive of men who take this option. Many smaller companies extend maternity leaves, but guarantee the mother her job or a comparable position only if favorable business conditions prevail. Most American companies that extend leaves do not give the mother any cash benefits after the immediate recovery period. Some corporations do allow the mother the option of returning to work on a part-time basis, and some allow mothers to adopt a flexitime schedule.

The bill (H.R. 4300) introduced in the House by Congress-woman Pat Schroeder of Colorado would require all companies to provide unpaid and job-protected leaves for eighteen weeks to new parents (including adoptive parents), disabled workers, and those needed at home to care for an ill child. Additionally, an employee could take up to eighteen weeks of unpaid leave over a twelve month period to recover from a serious health condition. Preexist- ing health benefits would continue during the leave. The employee would have a right to the same or an equivalent position upon returning to work. Both men and women are covered under the proposal. The bill would only apply to public or private employers with fifteen or more employees. This program would be modest by Western standards, but prospects even for its passage are problem- atical because a well-organized opposition is arguing that it would be too expensive for small to medium-size companies.

Schroeder's bill might have better prospects if it required em- ployers to pool their funds in an insurance plan that would cover the cost of parental leaves. There are several insurance options. One option would use the federally supervised unemployment-compensation program to cover parental leaves. A second would be state-managed insurance funds modeled on plans currently run by New York and New Jersey. A third option would require employers to obtain private insurance. Hawaii is currently the only state with such a law. Unless maternity/paternity leaves are financed through some type of insurance program, the protection and benefits that most parents receive in the immediate future will most likely depend upon the policies and wealth of their company.

An additional argument for establishing a national parental-leave policy in the United States is one of costs. Two experts on early child development and child care, Gamble and Zigler (1985), have estimated that the cost of high-quality infant and toddler day care is about $150 per week. Few families could afford these costs. If high standards are maintained, either employers or public agencies will have to supplement the costs for most families. A policy that allowed a parent to remain at home until a child was two might be less expensive. This would clearly be the case for parents with more than one preschooler.

Kamerman and Kahn (1987) argue that there are five steps in making parental leave a right without imposing a burdensome financial hardship on employers:

• All states should require employers to provide disability benefits to employees, including employees disabled by pregnancy and childbearing, and those required at home to care for an ill child. Coverage should be for a minimum of fourteen weeks every twenty-four months.

• All parents not covered by private medical insurance should be covered by public plans.

• All employees should be allowed to take a "parenting" or "child-care" leave, unpaid but job-protected, to devote time to child rearing.

• Employers should be encouraged to develop more part-time, flexitime, and phased-in work for new parents who want to balance child rearing with employment.

• Insurance "pools" should be developed to lower the costs of disability insurance for employers.

Family Planning and Sex Education

One of the most obvious ways to reduce poverty among women (especially young women) is to adopt policies that help them avoid unwanted and inopportune pregnancies. The evidence presented in chapter 4 showed that American teenagers of all races have a much higher rate of abortion and pregnancy than do teenagers in other Western industrial nations. This is true despite the fact that the level of sexual activity of American teenagers is about the same as that of teenagers in other Western countries (Weatherly 1988, 114). The difference is that other Western nations manifest more liberal attitudes toward sex and provide easier access to contraceptives and more comprehensive sex education.

Studies from the United States (SCCYF 1984b, 76) show that family planning education for teenagers is more successful if it is conducted within the school system and begins early in the teen years. A comprehensive approach might be based on in-school clinics that provide health counseling, including birth control information and contraceptives, employment counseling, and education on child care and parenting.

General funding by the federal government for family planning also needs to be increased. When President Reagan convinced Congress to cut funding for Title X (which financially assists health clinics that provide family planning assistance) in 1981, 1,000 of the 4,000 federally assisted clinics providing family planning services closed. The empirical evidence clearly reveals that this type of policy is dysfunctional. In fiscal years 1988 and 1989, Title X was allocated only $139.6 million and $138.0 million, respectively.

Sex education should be built into the education of all children and adolescents. Most school systems provide some sex education, but too often it consists of ten or fewer hours per year and is offered only in the later grades. One study has estimated that fewer than 10 percent of all schools offer comprehensive sex education courses of forty hours or more (Weatherley 1988, 130). Studies show that sex education does increase students' knowledge of sexuality, including use of contraceptives (Scales 1983). However, the evidence clearly shows that students exposed to sex education do not have higher levels of sexual activity (SCCYF 1984b, 37).

Educational Programs

There is probably no single strategy that could do more to break the cycle of poverty than ensuring quality education for all children. Unfortunately, current studies reveal that the education system fails many children. A recent study by the President's National Commission on Excellence in Education found that nearly 40 percent of all minority students are functional illiterates. The commission also found that nearly 40 percent of all students cannot draw inferences from written material, and one-third cannot solve a mathematical problem requiring more than two or three steps. Additionally, in many urban areas, 35 to 50 percent of all minority students drop out before graduation (SCCYF 1984b, 37).

As noted in chapter 4, the educational programs financed by the federal government make a positive but limited contribution. The federal programs do not achieve more because they are badly underfunded. Head Start serves only about 20 percent of the children qualified for admission by family income. Also, because of funding limitations, most of the children in the Head Start program attend school only part of the day. The federal assistance program to schools with large numbers of educationally deprived children (Education Consolidation and Improvement Act, Chapter 1) is also far too modest. The act provides about $600 a year per poor child. Most school districts use this money to hire remedial teachers, but the assistance is too low to allow the school systems to deal with the problem adequately.

While federal funding clearly needs to be increased, school

districts themselves must also do more. A 1989 study by the Committee for Economic Development, a policy research group financed by private business, recommended increased federal assistance plus a number of improvements by local districts. The study's recommendations included better training for teachers, with increased teacher salaries; more attention to low-income and poor-achieving students throughout their school years, with greatly increased attention to the junior high years; year-round schools to give students more attention, to extend child care, and give teachers better pay; and a common curriculum of English, math, science, and literature, monitored by periodic testing (Committee for Economic Development 1989; Grant Foundation 1988a, 1988b; LeCompte and Dworkin 1988, 162).

Job Programs and Benefits

There is clearly no solution to poverty in the United States without fundamental improvement in the employment status of millions of Americans. In the spring of 1988 the unemployment rate was 7.1 percent, little changed from the 7.5 percent rate when Ronald Reagan became president in 1980. A 7 percent unemployment rate translates into some 7.5 million unemployed Americans, not including another million or so who are too discouraged to continue to look for work (Bureau of the Census 1989b, 393; Ginsburg 1983, 29–30). The unemployment rate for minorities and teenagers is a great deal higher than the national average. In early 1988 black unemployment was 13 percent, 2.5 times the white rate. The Hispanic rate was 8.8 percent, 1.7 times the white rate. For black males twenty to twenty-four years old, the rate was 21.8 percent, and for black teenagers the rate was a staggering 34.7 percent (Button 1989).

As noted in earlier chapters, the high rate of poverty for minorities is often blamed on the breakdown of the family. But the very high rates of unemployment that prevail among young, minority males suggest that many families may break up or never form because a large percentage of these young men are in no position to support a family.

Unemployment is also a major problem of poor female household heads. In 1987 only 6.8 percent of poor female heads were employed full time, year round (Bureau of the Census 1987, 37). If poverty in the United States is to be reduced, major attention must be focused on the employment problems of young men and women who are single parents.

Although the employment problems of millions of Americans are severe, there are two facts that are quite positive. The first is that the population is aging, and over the next decade there will be fewer young people entering the job market. Specifically, the ratio of people age twenty-nine and under to those thirty to sixty-four is falling and will continue to decline until the mid-1990s (Easterlin 1980). This means that the number of new jobs that have to be created each year to lower unemployment will decline because young workers are new workers. A tighter labor market should also generate higher wages for young workers.

A second positive fact is that since the 1930s the United States has had a great deal of experience with employment programs (Harvey 1989). This experience has yielded two types of critical information. Empirical studies of the impact of various problems have identified the types of people who benefit most from programs, and the types of programs that work best (Barnow 1987; Bassi and Ashenfelter 1986; Beller 1980; Beyna, Bell, and Trutko 1984; Burtless 1989; Evanson 1984; Gueron 1986). The evidence indicates that youths with serious criminal records, former drug offenders, and adults with criminal records have been the least successful clientele (Hollister, Kemper, and Maynard 1984). Teenagers still in school, teenage dropouts without serious criminal records, and women welfare recipients have often benefited substantially from employment programs. The type of programs that work best are those tailored to a particular group that combine education, job training, confidence building, and the follow-up support required to allow the trainee to get established in the job market. Success is never easy, never cheap, and rarely dramatic, at least in the short run. But well-designed programs clearly produce positive results. A few of the programs that have proved worthwhile are reviewed below.

Programs for Teens and Young Adults

Two programs aimed at the one million unemployed youths age fifteen to twenty-four who have dropped out of school have produced positive results. The first is Job Corps, which has been in place since the early 1960s. This program uses an institutional approach. Teenagers and young adults live in a center away from their neighborhood where they are provided with remedial education and taught discipline and job skills. Currently there are 107 centers with about 60,000 trainees. Many of the young people have arrest records, and about two-thirds are minorities. About half of the centers are private for-profit and the rest are run by state or local governments. All centers are certified and supervised by the Department of Labor.

By 1987 about 1.3 million young people had graduated from the Job Corps (about one-third drop out before graduation). Of the graduates, 75 percent have obtained a job, returned to school, or joined the military. Cost estimates vary, but a nonprofit research institute in Princeton, New Jersey, estimates that the cost per student is about $6,244 and is recovered in taxes paid, reduced welfare costs, and lowered crime in about three years (Mallar et al. 1984; see also Thornton 1989, 334 n10).

The second program is Job Start. It is similar to Job Corps, but the participants live at home. They attend a school outside their neighborhood, where they receive educational assistance and job skills. Because housing is not provided, program costs are lower—about $4,000 per student. Early reports indicate that the program has been quite successful in the cities where it has been in place for several years (Manpower Demonstration Research Corporation [MDRC] 1985).

Another recent program that showed excellent results was the Youth Incentive Entitlements Pilot Projects initiated during the Carter administration. This program was aimed at the more than 2 million teenagers from low-income families who are still in school. The program was designed to get the students into the job market and to teach them how to be successful employees. Participating students were given a minimum-wage job on a full-time basis in the summer and part-time employment during the school year. They could keep the job only if they stayed in school and maintained their grades. Between 1978 and 1981 some 76,000 students were hired by private and public employers at seventeen sites across the nation.

An evaluation of the program by Rivlin (1984, 168–170) gave the program very high marks, especially where minority youth were concerned. Rivlin reported that when the program was made available, poor students—especially black youths—participated at a very high rate. Seventy-three percent of eligible black youths ages fifteen to sixteen years old participated, and the job incentive was successful in keeping them in school. Under the program the employment rate of black youths equaled that of white youths, and the black youths tended to stay on the job longer. Young black women had an employment rate one-third higher than that of young white women. The evidence from this study clearly suggests that the high unemployment rate of young blacks is not voluntary. Despite the positive impact of this program, the Reagan administration terminated it.

Programs for Welfare Recipients

A number of programs have had some success in assisting women on welfare. Some are inexpensive and have had a modest but positive impact on many recipients. An example is Job Search Workshops. This program is designed to help AFDC mothers learn about employment opportunities and receive instruction in successful job interviewing. Some programs also counsel the mothers on how they can obtain supportive services such as child care to help them get established in the job market (Burtless 1989, 126).

The Omnibus Budget Reconciliation Act (OBRA) of 1981 established three optional employment programs: the work incentive demonstration program (WIN), the community work experience program (CWEP), and the work supplementation program (Burtless 1989; Moffitt and Wolf 1987; Reischauer 1989; Thornton 1989). WIN was originally authorized in 1967 (Ketron, Inc. 1980). CWEP, generally called workfare, permitted states to require AFDC recipients to pay for their welfare checks by working. OBRA, however, allowed the states great latitude in setting up these programs.

As designed, CWEP never worked. Most AFDC recipients were exempt from CWEP, programs were limited in geographic scope within states, and those who participated were generally not required to work off their AFDC grant (GAO 1984). Many states and counties altered CWEP by providing pay in exchange for reduced benefits, financed support services such as child care, and often made the program voluntary. Workfare projects of some type were operational in twenty-three states in the mid-1980s. At least 518 counties were experimenting with the approach in the fall of 1985. Critics of CWEP argued that too often the programs were punitive in spirit, stigmatized the mother on the job, and failed to provide job training, supportive services, or job benefits.

Many who agreed with these criticisms of workfare nonetheless supported the adoption of some version of the program in their states. Some states designed programs that drew their inspiration from the third option—the better designed and financed Supported Work Demonstration (Burtless 1989; MDRC 1980). This program provided women who had been on AFDC for three or more years with job training and then helped them obtain a job. Child care was provided to dependent children. Between 1975 and 1980 some 10,000 welfare mothers participated in the program. Extensive evaluations have found considerable value in the program (Burtless 1989; Hollister, Kemper, and Maynard 1984; MDRC 1980). Two years after entering the job market, recipients received an estimated

$8,000 in benefits over costs. Compared to controls, the program participants had a 20 percent higher employment rate, worked 25 percent more hours, and earned almost 50 percent more. The best results were for women who were thirty-six to forty-four years of age at the beginning of their training. Many of the women in the program lost AFDC benefits, Medicaid, and food stamps. Thus, only about half of their earning gains were real, but they stayed in the program nonetheless.

In 1985 California instituted a highly publicized supported-work program. The California program provided job training and educational assistance, a reasonable salary, and child care. Other states established similar programs. Many of the states and counties experimenting with the program claimed success in placing welfare mothers in permanent jobs and substantially reducing welfare costs (Ellwood 1989; Friedlander, Erickson, Hamilton, and Knox 1986; Friedlander, Freedman, Hamilton, and Quint 1987; Friedlander, Hoerz, Long, and Quint 1985; Friedlander and Long 1987). Some of the programs, however, were clear failures (Burtless 1989, 120).

One of the most widely publicized supported-work programs has been in operation in Massachusetts since 1979. This program has two distinguishing features. First, welfare recipients are given job training or counseling and then placed in private sector jobs. The state has contracts with 6,000 private-sector employers. State officials felt that the traditional approach of placing the recipient in a public-sector job should be avoided because experience indicated that most never obtained a private-sector job. Second, child care is provided for a very small fee ($5 per week for two children) during the training period and while the mother works off the cost of her public assistance. After the mother leaves the welfare roles and while she is employed, child care is still provided at a subsidized rate (Ellwood 1989, 278).

Massachusetts trains welfare recipients to be employed as welders, construction workers, word processors, operating-room technicians, or high technology assemblers. The average pay for graduates of its programs has been over $6 an hour. State records show that 86 percent of the women placed in employment have stayed off welfare. Some 30,000 placements have been made, with a saving, after deducting the cost of the employment program, of $80 million to the state.

Other programs, including CETA, the Experimental Enrichment Program, and the AFDC Home Health Aide Demonstration, have also produced some positive results (Burtless 1989). Still, the limitations of these programs should be considered. The best gains have been made by women who volunteered for the program. Older women (in their thirties and forties) usually make more progress than young mothers. The well-financed programs that provide substantial training and supportive services produce the most positive results. The gains made by participants often result from longer work hours, not higher wages, and are usually not large enough to move participants over the poverty level or allow them to stay in the work force without supportive services such as health and child care (Burtless 1989; Walker 1989).

Walker (1989) points out that the limited success of these programs tend to result from inadequate funding, modest program goals, poor public-sector coordination, poor public–private-sector coordination, and failure of the programs to overcome illiteracy problems. The success of the Family Security Act of 1988 discussed below will depend in substantial measure on whether it is designed to overcome these problems.

Some Job Benefit Issues

To keep pace with women's changing roles there are a number of relatively small policies that, if adopted, could combine to help families considerably. From the early to the late-1980s a bipartisan group of lawmakers introduced in each session of Congress a package of bills known as the Economic Equity Act. This act included twenty-two measures designed to help women workers and single heads of households. The measures included:

• Allowing nonworking spouses to increase their contributions to individual retirement accounts.

• Allowing workers to qualify for retirement benefits after five years of work. Workers could aggregate several benefit packages into one during retirement years.

• Requiring couples to share Social Security benefits equally, even if one spouse does not work outside the home.

• Requiring companies to provide five years of health-care coverage to nonworking spouses after they are widowed or divorced.

• Raising the amount of income that a single-parent household can earn without paying taxes.

• Conducting a study of pay standards in the government to determine if there is sex-based discrimination.

As one of the primary sponsors of the bill, Pat Schroeder, said, this kind of legislation is necessary because the "real world no longer looks like a Norman Rockwell painting."

Altering the AFDC Program

When Congress decided not to support President Carter's welfare reform package, it brought to an end a debate that had extended over three administrations. After years of investigation and discussion, Congress had decided that fundamental reform of the welfare system should not be built on a negative income tax system. President Reagan consistently recommended reducing spending for current programs, but offered no substitute for them. During the mid-1980s Congress debated the Omnibus Anti-Poverty Act, which would have altered AFDC in some modest but significant ways. While this bill never passed Congress, it provided much of the foundation for significant reforms of AFDC passed by Congress in late 1988.

The Family Support Act of 1988

In October 1988 Congress agreed to amend the AFDC program significantly (Public Law 100-485, October 13, 1988, 102 Stat. 2343). The bill assumes that both parents should be responsible for the welfare of their children, and that the only escape from poverty for most poor female-headed families is supported employment. The goal is to reduce considerably the time that families remain dependent on AFDC. The revisions are designed to provide AFDC heads with the education, confidence, and job skills required by the labor force. To make employment a viable option, the bill finances child care for enrolled mothers. The bill also emphasizes improving child support from absent parents.

The provisions of the bill will be phased in over fiscal years 1989–1993. With a five-year cost of $3.3 billion, it will be too modest to impact poverty greatly. The provisions of the bill, however, are progressive and lay a foundation for much more substantial reform of the nation's welfare effort. There are five major provisions of the bill.

Title I. Child Support and Paternity

Starting in November 1990, states will be required to provide wage withholding of child support in all cases where the custodial parent receives public assistance or in those cases in which the custodial parent has asked for assistance in collecting child support. In 1994 states will be required to institute wage withholding of child support for almost all support orders. Child support awards will become more uniform as guidelines set the standards for all awards. These guidelines will be reviewed on a regular basis.

In fiscal 1992 the states will be penalized if they fail to establish paternity in a certain proportion of all cases of children born out of wedlock and receiving benefits. To help states locate missing parents, the bill provides access to both IRS and unemployment compensation data. A commission will be established to recommend ways to collect child support from noncustodial parents residing in a different state.

Title II. Job Opportunities and Basic Skills
Training Program (JOBS)

All states will be required to establish a JOBS program. All single parents with children over three (or at state option, over one) will be required to participate, unless they are ill, incapacitated, or have some other valid reason for nonparticipation. States will have a great deal of discretion in designing the programs, but they will have to be approved by Health and Human Services at least every two years. The JOBS program must be in place by October 1990 and statewide by October 1992. All welfare families must receive services. The state agency in charge of AFDC must assess the needs and skills of all AFDC heads. From this consultation an employability plan for each recipient will be developed specifying the activities the head will undertake and the supportive services the participant will receive.

The state programs must include education, job training, job preparedness training, and job placement. Postsecondary education and other approved employment activities may also be offered. Parents under age twenty without a high school diploma will be required to participate in an educational program leading to graduation. Demonstration projects will be carried out in up to five states to determine the advisability of providing education, job training, and placement to noncustodial parents.

In an effort to reduce long-term welfare dependency, the bill requires the states to spend at least 55 percent of all JOBS funds on (1) families that have received assistance for more than thirty-six months during the preceding five years; (2) families in which the head is under age twenty-four and has not completed high school; and (3) families that will lose benefits within two years because of the age of their children.

Title III. Supportive Services

The states will be required to provide child care to participants engaged in education, employment, or job training. To help recipients stay in the work force and leave the welfare roles, the state can assist in child care for up to one year. The cost of the care to the parent will be based on a sliding scale. Families leaving the AFDC ranks because of employment will be eligible for Medicaid coverage for up to one year.

Title IV. AFDC Amendments

The bill requires all the states to establish an AFDC-UP program. As noted in chapter 4, only about half the states currently have this program. By October 1990 all states must establish a program, but states new to the program may at their option limit benefits to a minimum of six months a year. However, Medicaid benefits would have to be ongoing.

The amount of money that an AFDC family can earn without reducing benefits will be raised to $90 a month from the current $75. The amount that a parent can spend on child care will be raised from $160 to $175 (or $200 if the child is under age 2). This expenditure for child care will not be counted as income in calculating AFDC benefits.

States may require single parents who are minors to reside with their parents or another guardian.

Title V. Demonstration Projects

The bill funds a rather wide range of innovative demonstration projects at the state level to determine how well various experimental programs alleviate problems or promote certain desirable outcomes. For example, $6 million over a three-year period is allocated to encourage innovative training and education programs for poor children. The sum of $3 million was authorized to fund programs to train poor family heads to be child-care providers. Eight million dollars was provided to establish programs to improve noncustodial parents' access to their children. Other programs will provide counseling for high-risk teenagers and incentives to businesses to create jobs for AFDC recipients.

The Impact of the Act

The Family Support Act will not reduce poverty in a major way over the next five years. The program is funded too modestly to impact a very large percentage of all AFDC recipients and it phases in rather slowly. Still, most poverty analysts would agree that it moves welfare reform in the right direction. The AFDC program will be more oriented toward helping the poor overcome barriers to self support. It will also have a preventive thrust because poor children will receive some of the assistance they need to become viable adults. These are critical steps toward reducing the incidence of poverty in America.

Increased Housing Assistance

Millions of low-income families are in need of housing assistance. In 1987 only 18 percent of all poor households received housing assistance from a federal, state, or local housing program (Leonard, Dolbeare, and Lazere 1989, 27). About one in five AFDC families received some type of housing assistance. Of those poor families with children who qualify as needy because they have incomes below the poverty level, or because their income is below 50 percent of the area median, only one in six receives any type of housing assistance (Ways and Means 1985, 245). In 1987 some 5.4 million poor renter households and at least 4 million poor families with children received no housing assistance (Leonard, Dolbeare, and Lazere 1989, 31).

Lack of housing assistance leaves millions of low-income families in inadequate or overcrowded housing and in undesirable neighborhoods. Additionally, it means that millions of low-income families must spend a disproportionate percentage of their total income on housing. Most studies conclude that housing costs in excess of 25 or 30 percent of income create serious financial burdens (CBO 1988; Stone 1983). A recent study by the federal government reported that over 70 percent of all poor households spend 30 percent or more of their total income for housing (Bureau of the Census 1989a, 4). Many of these families are suffering from ''shelter poverty.'' Their housing costs are so high that they cannot afford many of the basic necessities. The Bureau of Labor Statistics has calculated the minimum budget required for nonshelter items. The BLS figures show that a family of four with an income of $11,000 or less could not afford the basic necessities if they had any shelter costs (Stone 1983, 103–105).

Of all poor families, those headed by a single parent face the worst housing shortages and the highest cost burdens. In 1974 young single-parent families spent 46 percent of their total income on housing. By 1987 the cost of housing for these families rose to 81 percent of total income (Apgar and Brown 1989, 24). A recent study (Apgar and Brown 1989, 28) estimated that 24 percent of young single-parent households also lived in housing with moderate to severe physical deficiencies.

There are currently several major federal housing programs that assist families with children. All of these programs are limited to families with incomes below the poverty level for their family size or with a median income below 50 percent of the area average. Recipients pay 30 percent of their adjusted income toward the cost of the housing unit. The rent subsidy programs pay the difference between this amount and the fair-market value of the unit. Most of these programs are now known as Section 8 programs. Either the subsidy is paid directly to the landlord (certificate program) or the recipient receives a voucher that is redeemed by the landlord. The trend during the 1980s has been to convert most housing programs to these certificate or voucher programs.

There are still some 1.4 million units of public housing and about half are occupied by families with children (Burke 1984). In 1988 some 2.3 million units of housing were supported by Section 8 rent subsidies in existing or modestly rehabilitated housing or new or substantially rehabilitated housing. About half of these units are occupied by families with children. The various federal programs provide housing assistance to about 1.5 million low-income families with children.

The United States has never emphasized housing programs for low-income families. The inadequacy of housing programs has become increasingly apparent in recent years as the number of poor families has grown. Between 1979 and 1987 the number of poor families increased by over 30 percent. Measured by income, the poor also became poorer over this period (Leonard, Dolbeare, and Lazere 1989, 16). Despite the growth in poor families, the Reagan administration greatly reduced appropriations for housing. Appropriations dropped from a high of $32.3 billion in 1978 to approximately $10 billion in 1989 (CBO 1988).

As noted in chapter 5, most of the other major Western industrial nations make a much larger commitment to housing assistance than does the United States. In countries such as Sweden and West Germany, some 40 percent of all families qualify for housing assistance; in Great Britain, about 20 percent of all families live in publicly owned housing. The European countries place a special emphasis on providing housing assistance to low-income families with children, especially those headed by a single parent. Widely used policies in these countries include extensive housing allowances, public housing, home purchase grants, rehabilitation loans, building and saving subsidies, and the promotion and subsidy of a nonprofit market.

The budgetary constraints facing the United States in the next decade make it unlikely that Congress will greatly increase funding for housing programs. It could, however, hold the cost of housing assistance constant and still increase assistance to low-income families by altering the tax deduction system used to subsidize home owners. Under current tax policies which allow homeowners to deduct the cost of interest and taxes paid on their home or homes, the cost to the federal government in 1989 is estimated to be $53.2 billion in uncollected taxes (CBO 1988; Joint Committee on Taxation 1987). Families with incomes of $50,000 or more will receive 52.2 percent of these tax breaks (Leonard, Dolbeare, Lazere 1989, 33).

Housing assistance could be made much fairer by placing some limits on these tax deductions. An obvious option would be to limit the interest and tax deduction to some fixed dollar amount each year, and limit it to one home. Limiting the deduction to $30,000 in 1990, with a yearly adjustment for inflation, and limiting it to one home would increase federal tax revenues by several billion dollars a year. Even with this change, some 80 percent of all homeowners would still be able to deduct the full cost of the interest and tax expenses on their home. At current program costs, the funds generated by this change could be used to assist many of the low-income families with children who currently qualify for assistance but receive no aid.

Nutrition Programs

Meeting the nutritional needs of low-income people and families is relatively inexpensive. The total cost of all federal food programs was less than $20 billion in fiscal 1987. This includes the cost of the Food Stamp program, the nutrition pro-grant for Women, Infants, and Children (WIC), all school meal programs, and all commodity programs (Bureau of the Census 1987, 355). There is also considerable evidence that the various food programs have greatly reduced hunger and malnutrition in America since the mid-1960s (CBO 1980; Kotz 1979; Wellisch et al. 1983). However, notwithstanding the low cost of nutrition programs (especially compared to health-care costs), and the fact that the federal government spends huge amounts annually to store surplus (and perishable) farm commodities purchased from American farmers, the Reagan administration tightened eligibility for food programs and reduced federal outlays (Ways and Means 1985, 521–525). These cutbacks occurred when the number of poor was increasing more dramatically than in any other period since the 1950s. Not surprisingly, there is evidence of substantial increases in the incidence of hunger and malnutrition in recent years (Select Committee on Hunger 1985).

There are several deficiencies in current food programs that should be remedied. First, the evidence indicates that a significant percentage of all Food Stamp families run out of food before the end of the month (Kotz 1979, 21). This problem is especially acute in families with children. Second, many families who fall on hard times cannot receive food stamps because they are disqualified by asset limits. Third, in rural areas some families cannot obtain food stamps because they live far from the distribution centers (Kotz 1979, 19). Fourth, funding for the WIC program is so deficient that the program serves only one-third of the women qualified by income. Fifth, despite increased poverty, school meal programs served 3.2 million fewer children in 1986 than in 1979 (Bureau of the Census 1987, 355).

Expanding the Food Stamp, WIC, and school meal programs to correct these problems would cost less than $4 billion a year. This is not a small sum, but food programs do put money back into the economy and they lower health-care expenditures. One well-publicized federal study found that each $1 invested in WIC saved as much as $3 in short-term hospital costs (SCCYF 1985, 5; see also table 6.1). Thus, the net cost of food programs is much lower than outlays. Second, some nutrition problems could be met by a systematic distribution of government commodities. The Reagan administration distributed surplus commodities (especially cheese), but only episodically. A regular monthly distribution to low-income citizens would reduce government storage costs while helping millions of needy people.

Health Care

One of the most critical needs of low-income families is health-care assistance. The best estimates conclude that somewhere between 18 and 26 million Americans have no health insurance and another 37 million have only very limited coverage (CBO 1977a, 12–13; Social Security Administration 1985, 33). Recent surveys reveal that more than half of all poor children live in families with no private or public health-care coverage (Ways and Means 1985, 327). Equally critical, a survey by the Alan Guttmacher Institute concluded that 25 percent of all women of the prime childbearing age (eighteen to twenty-four) lack any type of medical coverage

Table 6.1

Cost-Effective Programs for Children

	Benefits for children	Cost benefit
WIC-special supplemental food program for women, infants, and children	Reduction in infant mortality and births of low birthweight infants.	$1 investment in prenatal component of WIC has saved as much as $3 in short-term hospital costs.
Prenatal care	Reduction in prematurity, low birthweight births, and infant mortality.	$1 investment can save $3.38 in cost of care for low birthweight infants.
Medicaid	Decreased neonatal and infant mortality and fewer abnormalities among children receiving Early Periodic Screening and Diagnostic Testing [EPSDT] services.	$1 spent on comprehensive prenatal care added to services for Medicaid's recipients has saved $2 in infant's first year; lower health-care costs for children receiving EPSDT services.
Childhood immunization	Dramatic declines in incidence of rubella, mumps, measles, polio, diptheria, tetanus, and pertussis.	$1 spent on Childhood Immunization Program saves $10 in later medical costs.

Preschool education	Increased school success, employability, and self-esteem; reduced dependence on public assistance.	$1 investment in quality preschool education returns $4.75 because of lower costs of special education, public assistance, and crime.
Compensatory education	Achievement gains and maintenance of gains in reading and mathematics.	Investment of $500 for year of compensatory education can save $3,000 cost of repeating grade.
Education for all handicapped	Increased number of students receiving services and more available services	Early educational intervention has saved school districts $1,560 per disabled pupil.
Youth employment and training	Gains in employability, wages, and success while in school and afterwards.	Job Corps returned $7,400 per participant, compared to $5,000 in program costs (in 1977 dollars). FY 1982 service year costs for YETP were $4,700; participants had annualized earnings gains of $1,810.

Source: Select Committee on Children, Youth, and Families (1985), "Opportunities for Success: Cost-Effective Programs for Children," House of Representatives, 99th Congress (Washington, D.C.: GPO), pp. 4–5.

(*New York Times* 1985c, 7). This same survey found that 11 percent of all women who work full time, 16 percent of those working for an hourly wage, and 24 percent of those working for small companies have no health insurance.

Meeting health-care needs is relatively expensive, at least in the short run. Health-care programs such as Medicaid are costly, but the evidence indicates that they have played a major role in reducing infant mortality rates and have improved the quality of health enjoyed by millions of recipients. The evidence is overwhelming that preventive health care pays for itself by reducing the incidence of serious, costly illness. It has been estimated, for example, that a complete prenatal treatment program costs about $600 (SCCYF 1984b, 27). By comparison, keeping a premature child in intensive care costs approximately $1,000 per day (table 6.1).

Health care could be extended to low-income families in a number of ways. One option would be to extend Medicaid coverage to all individuals living in households or families with incomes below the poverty level. Eligibility for Medicaid should be limited only by income, since linking eligibility to AFDC or SSI only forces people with medical needs to remain on the welfare rolls. A less attractive alternative would be to extend coverage to all children and pregnant women living in households or families with incomes below the poverty level.

Another approach that could be combined with expanded Medicaid coverage would be to increase the number of community health-care and migrant health-care centers. In 1985 there were 739 of these centers, serving about 5.5 million people a year. The centers provide free health care to persons at or below the poverty level, and reduced-cost care to other low-income patients. The centers cannot handle major medical problems and thus are not a total substitute for Medicaid. They can, however, take care of most of the health-care needs of recipients, and they are relatively cheap to finance. The centers in operation in 1985 were financed by payments from recipients, private insurance receipts, and subsidies by state and federal agencies.

Another option being discussed in some urban areas is for school districts to contract with health-maintenance organizations to handle the health-care needs of poor children. This option would provide a low-cost, comprehensive method of dealing with the health-care needs of children from low-income families.

Private industry will also have to do more. Employers should be required to provide employees and their families with decent health-care coverage. It would be financially advantageous for the federal government to subsidize HMOs that provide quality care at a reasonable cost to employees of small companies and nonprofit entities.

Summary and Conclusions

The data presented in chapters 1 and 2 show the changes in poverty demographics that have resulted in women and their dependent children becoming a majority of all the poor in America. The data also show that the fastest growing type of family in America is one headed by a single woman. This type of family is almost six times as likely to be poor as a family headed by a married couple. As single-parent families increase, poverty—especially for children—increases very significantly. In the early 1980s both the number of poor children and the rate of poverty for children were the highest since the early 1960s. During the 1980s poverty among children has averaged over 20 percent, making children the poorest age group in America. Currently more than half of all the poor and more than half of all poor children in America live in homes headed by single women.

The analysis in chapter 2 revealed that the rate of poverty for female-headed families has always been high, and that the rate has not changed dramatically over the last eighteen years. What has changed is the number of female-headed families. As this type of family has increased as a proportion of all families, the high rate of poverty for such families has greatly expanded the number of poor in female-headed households.

A number of factors have contributed to the increase in female-headed families, but the most important are rising rates of divorce, separation, and single parenting. All the evidence indicates that the number and proportion of all families headed by women will continue to grow. By the turn of the century, it can be expected that one out of four children will live in families headed by single women. The implications are obvious. Regardless of race, female-headed families tend to have low incomes (especially compared to male-headed and two-parent families) and high rates of unemployment. Welfare benefits do not come close to compensating for the income deficiencies of poor female-headed families, and in the 1980s these benefits have been steadily reduced. Some other types of social welfare programs, such as family planning services, have also been reduced and increasingly fail to reach the clients who need them most.

Statistical analysis reveals somewhat different correlates of poverty in black and white female-headed families. Black female-headed families often become the victims of poverty because of high rates of fertility, out-of-wedlock births, and divorce, combined with limited sources of income from employment, child support, and social welfare programs. The staggering rate of unemployment suffered by black males correlates strongly with the rate of poverty among black female-headed families. A causal relationship between the high rate of unemployment among black men and the high rates of divorce, abandonment, and out-of-wedlock births that cause much of the poverty in the black population seems apparent. The data suggest that white female-headed families fall into poverty because of increasing rates of divorce, high rates of unemployment, and limited sources of income, including inadequate social welfare services and child support.

Two major problems lie at the heart of increased rates of poverty among women. The first is the nation's continuing high rates of unemployment and subemployment for men and women. These problems are particularly severe for minority men. Second is the nation's failure to adapt its social policy to the changing role of women. This chapter has reviewed a range of nonwelfare policies and welfare reforms that could play a major role in addressing these two problems. The evidence reviewed suggests that state and federal governments can play a significant role in lowering the unemployment rate. The states could make a major contribution by assuring that public school students receive an academically sound education. Better academic programs and standards in the nation's public schools would increase the employment prospects of millions of young people. Additionally, job-training and job-placement programs can be designed to meet the needs of specific groups, such as minority teenagers and welfare mothers. The evidence clearly shows that teenagers, young adults, and welfare mothers are job-oriented and that they benefit significantly from well-designed programs. The cost of substantially reducing unemployment among these critical groups is quite reasonable, especially when discounted by the cost of broken homes and increased crime and welfare dependency.

Even women who work full time often earn less than they should because of wage disparities and pay discrimination. Issues of pay equity and sexual discrimination still need considerable attention.

Much of the poverty and economic deprivation that women and their dependent children suffer results from flaws in social programs. Inadequate and poorly enforced child-support laws create serious financial problems for millions of these families. Child-support statutes can be much better designed and enforced. Lack of decent, affordable child care also imposes hardships on millions of parents and children, often keeping mothers from working or receiving the education or job training they need to become employable. Private employers and public authorities can individually and in combination play a significant role in ameliorating this problem. The lack of a national maternity policy leaves mothers to the mercy and finances of their employers. A federal statute could establish guidelines for employers, and a combined state-federal program could subsidize employees who cannot obtain the needed assistance from their employer.

A number of federal policies could deal with many of the problems that create financial hardships for female-headed families. The federal commitment to family planning and sex education needs to be greatly expanded. The Earned Income Tax Credit can be amended in relatively minor ways to reduce substantially the tax burden on low-income families. Federal statutes could (1) improve the vestment rights of women who move in and out of the job market because of family responsibilities; (2) increase the IRA contribution of a nonworking spouse and make it tax deductable; (3) require that Social Security benefits be equally shared by a couple, regardless of the work record of each partner; and (4) obligate employers to cover the health-care needs of nonworking spouses for a set number of years after they are widowed or divorced.

The nation's major welfare programs are very badly flawed and in serious need of revision. The 1988 revisions in the AFDC program are positive, but too modestly financed. Additionally, the 1988 revisions in AFDC failed to establish a national minimum benefit level. This means that many states will continue to extend benefits that are so deficient that they will only exacerbate the problems of the poor. The nation also needs to accept responsibility for improving housing assistance, nutrition programs, and health care.

These reforms individually and in combination could play a role in greatly reducing the current rate of poverty among women and children. They would not be cheap, but they could be implemented for reasonable costs. Well-designed programs that substantially reduce poverty among women and children would in the long run pay for themselves many times over.

The federal government has a proven record of reducing poverty when it decides to do so. In 1959, 35.2 percent of all Americans age sixty-five and over lived in poverty. In 1987 the poverty rate for the aged was 12.2 percent. The rate dropped dramatically because expenditures for Social Security were increased and pegged to inflation, while most of the medical needs of the aged were covered by Medicare and Medicaid. The aged have learned the value of government assistance and are a well-organized lobby. In 1989 over 30 percent of the total federal budget consisted of expenditures for the aged. By contrast, less than 10 percent of the budget is devoted to programs for low-income families with children. Both the public and the private sectors need to recognize the gravity of the problems facing female-headed families, and each needs to do a great deal more to come to grips with it. The stakes are incalculable.

References

Alford, R. 1975. "Paradigms of Relations between State and Society." In *Stress and Contradiction in Modern Capitalism*, ed. L. Lindbery et al. Lexington, Mass.: Lexington Books.

Anderson, J. E., and Cope, L. G. 1987. "The Impact of Family Planning Program Activity on Fertility." *Family Planning Perspectives* 19: 152–157.

Apgar, W. C., and Brown, H. J. 1989. *The State of the Nation's Housing: 1988*. Cambridge, Mass.: The Joint Center for Housing Studies, Harvard University.

Bahr, S. J. 1979. "The Effects of Welfare on Marital Stability and Remarriage." *Journal of Marriage and the Family* 41 (August): 533–560.

Bane, M. J. 1976. *Here to Stay: American Families in the Twentieth Century*. New York: Basic Books.

Bane, M. J., and Ellwood, D. T. 1983. "The Dynamics of Dependency: The Routes to Self-Sufficiency." Cambridge, Mass.: Urban Systems Research and Engineering.

————. 1986. "Slipping into and out of Poverty: The Dynamics of Spells." *Journal of Resources* 21(1): 1–23.

Barnow, B. S. 1987. "The Impact of CETA Programs on Earnings: A Review of the Literature." *Journal of Human Resources* 22(2): 157–193.

Bassi, L. J., and Ashenfelter, O. 1986. "The Effect of Direct Job Creation and Training Programs on Low-Skilled Workers." In *Fighting Poverty: What Works and What Doesn't*, ed. S. Danziger and D. H. Weinberg. Cambridge, Mass.: Harvard University Press.

Becker, G. S. 1981. *A Treatise on the Family*. Cambridge, Mass.: Harvard University Press.

Beckerman, W. 1979. "The Impact of Income Maintenance Payments on Poverty in Britain, 1975." *The Economic Journal* (June): 261–279.

167

Beller, A. H. 1980. "The Effect of Economic Conditions on the Success of Equal Employment Opportunity Laws." *The Review of Economics and Statistics* 62 (August).
————. 1982. "Occupational Segregation by Sex: Determinants and Changes." *The Journal of Human Resources* 17(3) Summer.
Bergman, B. 1974. "Occupational Segregation, Wages and Profits When Employers Discriminate by Race or Sex." *Eastern Economic Journal* 1 (April): 103–110.
————. 1989. "Does the Market for Women's Labor Need Fixing?" *Journal of Economic Perspectives* 3(1) Winter: 43–60.
Berrueta-Clement, J. R. et al. 1984. *Changed Lives: The Effects of the Perry Preschool Program on Youths Through Age 19.* Ypsilanti, Mich.: High Scope Educational Research Foundation.
Berry, J. 1984. *Feeding Hungry People: Rulemaking in the Food Stamp Program.* New Brunswick, N.J.: Rutgers University Press.
Beyna, L.; Bell, J.; and Trutko, J. 1984. *Six Month Evaluation of the Maryland Day Care Voucher Demonstration.* Arlington, Va.: James Bell and Associates.
Bianchi, S., and Farley, R. 1979. "Racial Differences in Family Living Arrangements and Economic Well-Being: An Analysis of Recent Trends." *Journal of Marriage and the Family* 41 (August): 537–551.
Bixby, A. K. 1989. "Public Social Welfare Expenditures, Fiscal Year 1986." *Social Security Bulletin* 52(2): 29–39.
Blank, H., and Wilkins, A. 1986. *State Child Care Fact Book 1986.* Washington, D.C.: Children's Defense Fund.
Blau, D. M., and Robins, P. K. 1988. "Child-Care Costs and Family Labor Supply." *The Review of Economics and Statistics* 70(3) August: 374–381.
Brookes, S. 1988. "Europe's Job Crisis: Here to Stay," *Europe* (May): 34–35.
Brown, B. 1977. "Long-Term Gains from Early Intervention: An Overview of Current Research." Paper presented at the 1977 Annual Meeting of the American Association for the Advancement of Sciences, Denver, Colo.
Bumpass, L. 1984. "Children and Marital Disruption: A Replication and an Update." *Demography* 21 (February): 71–82.
Bumpass, L., and Rindfuss, R. R. 1979. "Children and the Experience of Marital Disruption." *American Journal of Sociology* 85 (July): 49–65.
Bureau of the Census. 1976. "Number, Timing, and Duration of Marriages and Divorce in the United States: June 1975." *Current Population Reports.* Series P–20, no. 297. Washington, D.C.: GPO.
————. 1979. *Statistical Abstract of the United States 1979.* 100th ed. Washington, D.C.: GPO.
————. 1980a. "Child Support and Alimony: 1978." *Current Population Reports.* Special Studies Series P–23, no. 106, Advance Report. Washington, D.C.: GPO.
————. 1980b. *Statistical Abstract of the United States 1980.* 101st ed. Washington, D.C.: GPO.
————. 1981a. "Characteristics of Households and Persons Receiving Noncash

Benefits." *Current Population Reports*. Series P–32, no. 110. Washington, D.C.: GPO.

―――. 1981b. "Current Housing Reports, Annual Housing Survey: 1980, Part C, Financial Characteristics of the Housing Inventory, U.S. Regions." Series H15–80. Washington, D.C.: GPO.

―――. 1981c. *Statistical Abstract of the United States 1981*. 102d ed. Washington, D.C.: GPO.

―――. 1982a. "Child Care Arrangements of Working Mothers: June 1982." *Current Population Reports*. Series P–23, no. 129. Washington, D.C.: GPO.

―――. 1982b. "Fertility of American Women: June 1981." *Current Population Reports*. Series P–20, no. 369. Washington, D.C.: GPO.

―――. 1982c. "Population Profiles of the United States: 1981." *Current Population Reports*. Series P–20, no. 374. Washington, D.C.: GPO.

―――. 1983. *Statistical Abstract of the United States 1984*. 104th ed. Washington, D.C.: GPO.

―――. 1984. "Economic Characteristics of Households in the United States: First Quarter 1984." *Current Population Reports*. Series P–70, no. 3. Washington, D.C.: GPO.

―――. 1985a. "Money Income and Poverty Status of Families and Persons in the United States: 1984." *Current Population Reports*. Series P–60, no. 149. Washington, D.C.: GPO.

―――. 1985b. "Economic Characteristics of Households in the United States: First Quarter, 1984." *Current Population Reports*. Series P–70, no. 3. Washington, D.C.: GPO.

―――. 1986. "Economic Characteristics of Households in the United States: Fourth Quarter, 1985," *Current Population Reports*. Series P–70, no. 6: 24–25. Washington, D.C.: GPO.

―――. 1987. *Statistical Abstract of the United States 1988*. 108th ed. Washington, D.C.: GPO.

―――. 1988a. "Money Income and Poverty Status of Families and Persons in the United States: 1987." *Current Population Reports*. Series P–60, No. 161. Washington, D.C.: GPO.

―――. 1988b. *An Aging World*. International Population Reports. Series P–95, No. 78. Washinton, D.C.: GPO.

―――. 1989a. "American Housing Survey, 1985." U.S. Department of Housing and Urban Development. Washington, D.C.: GPO.

―――. 1989b. *Statistical Abstract of the United States 1989*. 109th ed., Washington, D.C.: GPO.

Burke, V. 1984. "Cash and Non-Cash Benefits for Persons with Limited Income: Eligibility Rules, Recipient and Expenditure Data: FY 1981–83." Report no. 84–99. Washington, D.C.: Congressional Research Service.

Burke, V.; Gabe, T.; Rimkunas, R.; and Griffith, J. 1985. *Hispanic Children in Poverty*. Report no. 85–170. Washington, D.C.: Congressional Research Service.

Burlage, D. 1978. "Divorced and Separated Mothers: Combining the Responsibilities of Breadwinning and Child Rearing." Ph.D. dissertation, Harvard University.

Burnham, W. D. 1980. "American Politics in the 1980s." *Dissent* (Spring): 152–157.

Burstein, P. 1979. "Equal Employment Opportunity Legislation and the Income of Women and Nonwhites." *American Sociological Review* 44 (June): 367–391.

Burt, M. 1986. "Estimates of Public Costs for Teenage Childbearing." Unpublished paper prepared for the Center for Population Options, Washington. D.C.

Burtless, G. 1989. "The Effect of Reform on Employment, Earnings and Income." In *Welfare Policy for the 1990s*, ed. P. H. Cottingham and D. T. Ellwood, 103–140. Cambridge, Mass.: Harvard University Press.

Burud, S.; Aschbacher; and McCoskey, J. 1984. *Employer-Supported Child Care: Investing in Human Resources*. Dover, Mass.: Auburn House.

Business Week. 1985. "The Forgotten Americans." September 2, pp. 50–55.

Button, J. W. 1989. *Blacks and Social Change: Impact of the Civil Rights Movement in Southern Communities*. Princeton, N.J.: Princeton University Press.

Cairncross, F. 1988. "European Countries Vary Widely in Health-Care Delivery Systems." *Financier: The Journal of Private Sector Policy* 12: 10–13.

Carlson, E., and Stinson, K. 1982. "Motherhood, Marriage Timing, and Marital Stability: A Research Note." *Social Forces* 61 (September): 258–267.

Center for the Study of Social Policy. 1984. "Working Female-Headed Families in Poverty: Three Studies of Low-Income Families Affected by the AFDC Policy Changes in 1981." Washington, D.C.

Chafe, W. H. 1972. *The American Woman: Her Changing Social, Economic and Political Role, 1920–1970*. New York: Oxford University Press.

Chafetz, J. S. 1984. *Sex and Advantage: A Comparative Macro-Structural Theory of Sex Stratification*. Totowa, N.J.: Rowman and Allanheld.

Cherlin, A. 1980 "Postponing Marriage: The Influence of Young Women's Work Expectations." *Journal of Marriage and the Family* 42 (May): 355–365.

———. 1981. *Marriage, Divorce, and Remarriage*. Cambridge, Mass: Harvard University Press.

Children's Defense Fund. 1984. "The Deficit Reduction Act of 1984." Washington, D.C.

———. 1987. *Child Care: The Time Is Now*. Washington, D.C.

Cicirelli, V. G., et al. 1977. *The Impact of Head Start: An Evaluation of the Effects of Head Start on Children's Cognitive and Affective Development*. Ohio University, Columbus: Westinghouse Learning Corporation.

Citizens' Board of Inquiry into Hunger and Malnutrition in the United States. 1968. *Hunger, USA*. Boston: Beacon.

Clarke-Stewart, A. 1982. *Daycare*. Cambridge, Mass.: Harvard University Press.

Clayton, R. R., and Voss, H. L. 1977. "Shacking Up: Cohabitation in the 1970s." *Journal of Marriage and the Family* 39 (May): 273–283.

Cocoran, M., and Duncan, G. 1979. "Work History, Labor Force Attachment, and Earnings Differences between Races and Sexes." *Journal of Human Resources* 14 (Winter): 3–20.

Cole, S.; Danziger, S.; and Piliavin, I. 1983. "Poverty and Welfare Recipiency after OBRA: Some Preliminary Evidence from Wisconsin." University of Wisconsin, Madison, Institute for Research on Poverty.

Commission of the European Communities. 1981. Final Report from the Commissioners to the Council on the First Programme of Pilot Scheme and Studies to Combat Poverty. Brussels.

————. 1982. *One-Parent Families and Poverty in the EEC*. Copenhagen.

Committee for Economic Development. 1989. *Children in Need: Investment Strategies for the Educationally Disadvantaged*. Washington, D.C.: CED.

Committee on Ways and Means. 1985. *Children in Poverty*. U.S. House of Representatives, 99th Congress, 1st Session. Washington, D.C.: GPO.

Congressional Budget Office. 1977a. *Catastrophic Health Insurance*. Washington, D.C.: GPO.

————. 1977b. *The Food Stamp Program: Income or Food Supplementative?* Washington, D.C.: GPO.

————. 1980. *Feeding Children: Federal Child Nutrition Policies in the 1980s*. Washington, D.C.: GPO.

————. 1983. "Major Legislative Changes in Human Resources Programs since January 1981." Staff memorandum, August.

————. 1989. *Current Housing Problems and Possible Federal Responses*. Washington, D.C.: GPO.

Congressional Quarterly Weekly Report. 1982. "For the Poor, A Wait for Better Housing." (December 4).

Consortium for Longitudinal Studies. 1978. *Lasting Effects After Preschool*. Final Report of DHEW Grant No. 90C–1311. Washington, D.C., U.S. Administration for Children, Youth, and Families.

Cook, A. H. 1989. "Public Policies to Help Dual-Earner Families Meet the Demands of the Work World." *Industrial and Labor Relations Review* 48: 201–215.

Cooney, R. S. 1979. "Demographic Components of Growth in White, Black and Puerto Rican Female-Headed Families: Comparison of the Cutright and Ross Sawhill Methodologies." *Social Research* 8 (June): 144–158.

Cottingham, C., ed. 1982. *Race, Poverty, and the Urban Underclass*. Lexington, Mass.: Lexington Books.

Cottingham, P. H., and Ellwood, D. T., eds. 1989. *Welfare Policy for the 1990s*. Cambridge, Mass.: Harvard University Press.

Cramer, J. C. 1980. "Fertility and Female Employment." *American Sociological Review* 47 (August): 556–567.

Cutright, P. 1974. "Components of Change in the Number of Female Family Heads Aged 15–44: U.S., 1940–70." *Journal of Marriage and the Family* 36 (November): 714–721.

Danziger, S. 1981. "Post-Program Changes in the Lives of AFDC Supported Work Participants: A Quantitative Assessment." *Journal of Human Resources* 16 (April): 31–42.

————. 1982. "Children in Poverty: The Truly Needy Who Fall through the Safety Net." *Children and Youth Services*, 35–51.

————. 1984. "The Impact of the Reagan Budget Cuts on Working Welfare Mothers in Wisconsin." *Challenge* 27 (November): 763–784.

————. 1989. "Fighting Poverty and Reducing Welfare Dependency." In *Welfare Policies for the 1990s*, ed. P. H. Cottingham and D. T. Ellwood, 41–69. Cambridge, Mass.: Harvard University Press.

Danziger. S., and Gottschalk, P. 1985. "The Poverty of Losing Ground." *Challenge* 28 May/June: 32–38.

————. 1988–1989. "Increasing Inequality in the United States: What We Know and What We Don't." *Journal of Post Keynesian Economics*, 11, 2: 174–195.

Danziger, S.; Gottschalk, P.; and Smolensky, E. 1989. "How the Rich Have Fared, 1973–1987." *The American Economic Review* 79(2) May: 310–314.

Danziger, S., and Haveman, R. 1981. "The Reagan Administration's Budget Cuts: Their Impact on the Poor," *Challenge* 24 (May-June): 5–13.

Department of Labor. 1984. "Analysis of Job Training, Longitudinal Survey with Turn Around Data: JTPA Title II-A (October 1983–March 1984)."

DeSario, J. P., ed. 1989. *International Public Policy Sourcebook*. Westport, Conn.: Greenwood Press.

Downes, B. T. 1968. "Social and Political Characteristics of Riot Cities: A Comparative Study." *Social Science Quarterly* 49 (December): 509–520.

Dubnoff, S. 1986. "Work Related Day Care: A Survey of Parents." *FY '86 Day Care Report*. Boston: Massachusetts Department of Social Services.

Duncan, G. J., and Ponza, M. 1987. "Public Attitudes toward the Structure of Income Maintenance Programs." University of Michigan, Ann Arbor, Survey Research Center. Working paper.

Duncan, G. J., and W. L. Rodgers. 1988. "Longitudinal Aspects of Childhood Poverty." *Journal of Marriage and Family*, forthcoming.

Duvall, L. J.; Gondreau, D. W.; and Marsh, R. E. 1982. "Aid to Families with Dependent Children: Characteristics of Recipients in 1979." *Social Security Bulletin* 45(4) April: 1, 6.

Easterlin, R. 1980. *Birth and Fortune: The Impact of Numbers on Personal Wealth*. New York: Basic Books.

Ellwood, D. T. 1986. "Targeting Would-Be Long-Term Recipients of AFDC." Princeton, N.J.: Mathematica Policy Research, Inc.

————. 1988. *Poor Support: Poverty in the American Family*. New York: Basic Books.

————. 1989. "Conclusions." In *Welfare Policy for the 1990s*, ed. P.H. Cottingham and D. T. Ellwood, 269–290. Cambridge, Mass.: Harvard University Press.

Ellwood, D. T., and Bane, M. J. 1985. "The Impact of AFDC on Family Structure and Living Arrangements." *Research in Labor Economics* 7: 137–149.

Espenshade, T. J. 1979. "The Economic Consequences of Divorce." *Journal of Marriage and Family* 41 (August): 615–625.

Evanson, E. 1984. "Employment Programs for the Poor: Government in the Labor Market." *Focus* 7(3) Fall: 1–7.

Feagin, J. R. 1975. *Subordinating the Poor: Welfare and American Beliefs.* Englewood Cliffs, N.J.: Prentice-Hall.

Fester, D.; Gottschalk, P.; and Jakubson, G. 1984. "Impact of OBRA on AFDC Recipients in Wisconsin." Madison: Institute for Research on Poverty. Discussion paper no. 763–84 (November).

Finer, M., et al. 1974. *Report on the Committee on One-Parent Families.* London: Her Majesty's Stationery Office.

Flora, P., and Heidenheimer, A. J., eds. 1981. *The Development of Welfare States in Europe and America.* New Brunswick, N.J: Transaction.

Ford Foundation. 1989. *The Common Good: Social Welfare and the American Future.* New York: Ford Foundation.

Forest, J. D.; Hermalin, A. I.; and Henshaw, S. K. 1981. "The Impact of Family Planning Clinic Programs on Adolescent Pregnancy." *Family Planning Perspectives* 13: 3–12.

Fosburg, S., and Hawkins, P. 1981. *Final Report of the National Day Care Home Study,* Vol. 1. Cambridge, Mass.: ABT Books.

Freeman, J. 1975. *The Politics of Women's Liberation.* New York: Longman.

Friedlander, D.; Erickson, M.; Hamilton, G.; and Knox, V. 1986. *West Virginia: Final Report on the Community Work Experience Demonstration.* New York: Manpower Demonstration Research Corporation.

Friedlander, D.; Freedman, S.; Hamilton, G.; and Quint, J. 1987. *Final Report on the Illinois WIN Demonstration Program in Cook Country.* New York: Manpower Demonstration Research Corporation.

Friedlander, D.; Hoerz, G.; Long, D.; and Quint, J. 1985. *Maryland: Final Report on the Employment Initiatives Evaluation.* New York: Manpower Demonstration Research Corporation.

Friedlander, D., and Long, D. 1987. *A Study of Performance Measures and Subgroup Impacts in Three Welfare Employment Programs.* New York: Manpower Demonstration Research Corporation.

Friedman, D. E. 1986. "Child Care For Employees' Kids." *Harvard Business Review* March-April: 28–34.

Fuchs, V. 1981. *How We Live.* Cambridge, Mass: Harvard University Press.

———. 1989. "Women's Quest for Economic Equality." *Journal of Economic Perspectives* 3(1) Winter: 25–41.

Furniss, N., and Mitchell, N. 1984. "Social Welfare Provisions in Western Europe: Current Status and Future Possibilities." In *Public Policy and Social Institutions,* ed. H. Rodgers. Greenwich, Conn.: JAI Press.

Furniss, N., and Tilton, T. 1979. *The Case for the Welfare State: From Social Security to Social Equality.* Bloomington: Indiana University Press.

Furstenberg, F. F., Jr. 1976. *Unplanned Parenthood: The Social Consequences of Teenage Childbearing.* New York: Free Press.

Furstenberg, F. F., Jr.; Lincoln, R.; and Menken, J. 1981. *Teenage Sexuality, Pregnancy, and Childbearing*. Philadelphia: University of Pennsylvania Press.

Gamble, T., and Zigler, E. 1985. "Effects of Infant Day Care: Another Look at the Evidence." *American Journal of Orthopsychiatry* 56: 26–42.

Garfinkel I., and McLanahan, S. 1986. *Single Mothers and Their Children: A New American Dilemma*. Washington, D.C.: Urban Institute.

Garfinkel, I.; McLanahan S.; and Wong. P. 1988. "Child Support and Dependency." In *Beyond Welfare: New Approaches to the Problem of Poverty in America*, ed. H. R. Rodgers, Jr., Armonk, N.Y.: M. E. Sharpe.

Garfinkel, I., and Uhr, E. 1984. "A New Approach to Child Support," *The Public Interest* 75 (Spring): 111–122.

General Accounting Office. 1980. *Better Management and More Resources Needed to Strengthen Federal Efforts to Improve Pregnancy Outcomes*. Washington, D.C.: GPO.

———. 1984. *CWEP's Implementation Results to Date Raise Questions about the Administration's Proposed Mandatory Work Program*. (PEMD–84–2). Washington, D.C.: GAO Program Evaluation and Methodology.

———. 1987. *Work and Welfare: Current AFDC Work Programs and Implications for Federal Policy*. Report HRD–87–34. Washington, D.C.: GAO.

Gilder, G. 1981. *Wealth and Poverty*. New York: Bantam.

Ginsburg, H. 1983. *Full Employment and Public Policy: The United States and Sweden*. Lexington, Mass.: Lexington Books.

Glick, P. C., and Spanier, G. B. 1980. "Married and Unmarried Cohabitation in the United States." *Journal of Marriage and the Family* 42 (February): 19–30.

Gold, M. E. 1983. *A Dialogue on Comparable Worth*. New York: ILR Press, New York State School of Industrial and Labor Relations, Cornell Univer-sity.

Goldman, B.; Friedlander, D.; and Long D. 1986. *Final Report on the San Diego Job Search and Work Experience Demonstration*. New York: Manpower Demonstration Research Corporation.

Gottschalk, P. 1981. "Transfer Scenarios and Projections of Poverty into the 1980s." *Journal of Human Resources* 16: 41–60.

Grant Foundation. 1988a. *The Forgotten Half: Non-College Youth in America*. Washington, D.C.: W. T. Grant Foundation.

———. 1988b. *The Forgotten Half: Pathways to Success for America's Youth and Young Families*. Washington, D.C.: W. T. Grant Foundation.

Gueron, J. M. 1986. *Work Initiatives for Welfare Recipients: Lessons from a Multi-State Experience*. New York: Manpower Demonstration Research Corporation.

Gutmann, A., ed. 1988. *Democracy and the Welfare State*. Princeton, N.J.: Princeton University Press.

Guttentag, M., and Secord, P. 1983. *Too Many Women: The Sex Ratio Question*. Beverly Hills, Calif.: Sage.

Haanes-Olsen, L. 1989. "Worldwide Trends and Developments in Social Security, 1985–87." *Social Security Bulletin* 52(2). Washington, D.C.: Department of Health and Human Services.

Hahn, L. H., and Feagin, J. R. 1970. "Rank-and-File Versus Congressional Perceptions of Ghetto Riots." *Social Science Quarterly* 51 (September): 361–373.

Hallett, G., ed. 1988. *Land and Housing Policies in Europe and the USA: A Comparative Analysis.* New York: Routledge.

Hannan, M. T.; Tuma, N. B.; and Groeneveld, P. 1977. "Income and Marital Events: Evidence from the Income Maintenance Experiment." *American Journal of Sociology* 82 (May): 1186–1211.

Hanson, R. L. 1983. "The 'Content' of Welfare Policy: The States and Aid to Families with Dependent Children." *Journal of Politics* 45: 771–785.

———. 1984. "Medicaid and the Politics of Redistribution." *American Journal of Political Science* 28: 313–339.

Harvey, P. 1989. *Securing the Right to Employment: Social Welfare Policy and the Unemployed in the United States.* Princeton, N.J.: Princeton University Press.

Hayes, C., ed. 1987. *Risking the Future: Adolescent Sexuality, Pregnancy, and Childbearing.* Washington, D.C.: National Academy Press.

Headey, B. 1978. *Housing Policy in the Developed Economy: The United Kingdom, Sweden, and the United States.* London: Croom Helm.

Hertzke, A. D., and Scribner, M. K. 1989. "The Politics of Federal Day Care: The Nexus of Family, Church, and the Positive State." Prepared for delivery at the Annual Meeting of the American Political Science Association, Atlanta, August 31, 1989.

Hofferth, S., and Moore, K. 1979. "Early Childbearing and Later Economic Well-being." *American Sociological Review* 44 (October): 784–815.

Hofferth, S., and Phillips, D. A. 1987. "Child Care in the United States: 1970 to 1985." *Journal of Marriage and Family* 49: 559–571.

Hollister, R. G.; Kemper, P.; and Maynard, R. A., eds. 1984. *The National Supported Work Demonstration.* Madison: University of Wisconsin Press.

Houston Chronicle. 1985a. "Many States Now Offer Work Fare." October 13, p. 24.

Houston Chronicle. 1985b. "Schools Failing U.S. Business, Report Charges." September 6, p. 18.

Human Resources Administration. 1983. "Effects of Federal Budget Cutbacks on Employed ADC Parents." New York: City of New York.

Hutchens, R. 1984. "Changing the AFDC Program: The Effects of the Omnibus Budget Reconciliation Act of 1981." Institute for Research on Poverty. Discussion Paper no. 764–84 (December).

Institute for Research on Poverty. 1985. "Measuring the Effects of the Reagan Welfare Changes on the Work Effort and Well-Being of Single Parents." *Focus* 8(1): 1–5.

Jackson, J. J. 1973. "Black Women in a Racist Society." In *Racism and Mental Health,* ed. C.V. Willie, B. M. Kramer, and B. S. Brown. Pittsburgh: University of Pittsburgh Press.

Johansen, E. 1984. *Comparable Worth: The Myth and the Movement.* Boulder, Colo.: Westview Press.

Joint Committee on Taxation. 1987. *Estimates of Federal Tax Expenditures for Fiscal Years 1988–1992*. U.S. Congress.

Jones, E. F., et al. 1985. "Teenage Pregnancy in Developed Countries: Determinants and Policy Implications." *Family Planning Perspectives* 17 (March–April): 53–63.

Kahn, A. J. 1983. *Income Transfers for Families with Children: An Eight-County Study*. Philadelphia: Temple University Press.

———. 1987. *Child Care: Facing the Hard Choices*. Dover, Mass.: Auburn House.

———. 1988. *Child Support: From Debt Collection to Social Policy*. Beverly Hills, Calif.: Sage.

Kamerman, S. B. 1980. *Maternity and Parental Benefits and Leaves: An International Review*. New York: Columbia University Press.

———. 1984. "Women, Children and Poverty: Public Policies and Female-headed Families in Industrialized Countries." *Signs: Journal of Women in Culture and Society* 10(21): 249–271.

———. 1988. *Mothers Alone: Strategies for a Time of Change*. Dover, Mass.: Auburn House.

———. 1989. *Privatization and the Welfare State*. Princeton, N.J.: Princeton University Press.

Kamerman, S. B., and Kahn, A. J. 1981. *Child Care, Family Benefits, and Working Parents*. New York: Columbia University Press.

———. 1983. "Child Support: Some International Developments." In *Parental Support Obligations*, ed. J. Cassetty. Lexington, Mass.: Lexington Books.

———. 1987. Quoted in *Ms.*, March, p. 44.

———. 1988. "What Europe Does for Single-Parent Families." *Public Interest* (Fall): 70–86.

Katz, M. B. 1986. *In the Shadow of the Poorhouse: A Social History of Welfare in America*. New York: Basic Books.

Kessler-Harris, A. 1982. *Out to Work—A History of Wage-Earning Women in the United States*. New York: Oxford University Press.

Ketron, Inc. 1980. *The Long-Term Impact of WIN II: A Longitudinal Evaluation of the Employment Experiences of Participants in the Work Incentive Program*. Report. Wayne, Penn.: Ketron, Inc.

Keyserling, M. 1972. *Windows on Day Care*. New York: National Council of Jewish Women.

Kimmich, M. 1984. *Children's Services in the Reagan Era*. Washington, D.C.: Urban Institute.

King, A. G. 1978. "Labor Market Racial Discrimination against Black Women." *The Review of Black Political Economy* 8(4) Summer: 116–131.

Korbin, K. E. 1973. "Household Headship and Its Changes in the United States, 1940–1960, 1970." *Journal of the American Statistical Association* 68 (December): 793–800.

Kotz, N. 1971. *Let Them Eat Promises: The Politics of Hunger in America*. New York: Doubleday.

————. 1979. *Hunger in America: The Federal Response*. New York: Field Foundation.

Lantz, H.; Martin, S.; and O'Hara, M. 1977. "The Changing American Family from the Preindustrial to the Industrial Period: A Final Report." *American Sociological Review* 42 (June): 406–421.

Lasch, K. C. 1980. "Life in the Therapeutic State." *New York Review of Books* 27 (June 12): 24–32.

LeCompte, M. D., and Dworkin, A. G. 1988. "Educational Programs: Indirect Linkages and Unfulfilled Expectations." In *Beyond Welfare: New Approaches to the Problem of Poverty in America*, ed. H. R. Rodgers, Jr., 135–167. Armonk, N.Y.: M. E. Sharpe, Inc.

Leichter, H. M. 1979. *A Comparative Approach to Policy Analysis; Health Care Policy in Four Nations*. New York: Cambridge University Press.

Leichter, H. M., and Rodgers, H. R., Jr. 1984. *American Public Policy in a Comparative Context*. New York: McGraw-Hill.

Leman, C. 1977. "Patterns of Policy Development: Social Security in the United States and Canada." *Public Policy* 25 (Spring): 261–291.

Leonard, P. A.; Dolbeare, C. N.; and Lazere, E. B. 1989. *A Place to Call Home: The Crisis in Housing for the Poor*. Washington, D.C.: Center on Budget and Policy Priorities and Low Income Housing Information Service.

Lerman, R. I. 1989. "Child-Support Policies." In *Welfare Policy for the 1990s*, ed. P. H. Cottingham and D. T. Ellwood, 219–247. Cambridge, Mass.: Harvard University Press.

Levitan, S.; Rein, M.; and Marwick, D. 1972. *Work and Welfare Go Together*. Baltimore: Johns Hopkins Press.

Levy, F. 1980. "Labor Force Dynamics and the Distribution of Employability." Washington, D.C.: Urban Institute.

Lindbeck, A. 1988. "Consequences of the Advanced Welfare State." *World Economy* 11: 19–37.

Lloyd, C. B., and Niemi, B. T. 1979. *The Economics of Sex Differentials*. New York: Columbia University Press.

Magid, R.Y. 1983. *Child Care Initiatives for Working Parents: Why Employers Get Involved*. New York: American Management Association.

Mahler, V. A., and Claudio, J. K. 1988. "Social Benefits in Advanced Capitalist Countries: A Cross-National Comparison." *Comparative Politics* 21: 37–51.

Mahler, V. A., and Katz, C. J. 1988. "Social Benefits in Advanced Capitalist Countries." *Comparative Politics* 43: 37–51.

Mallar, C., et al. 1984. *The Lasting Impact of Job Corps Participation*. Princeton, N.J.: Mathematica.

Mann, A. J. 1977. "A Review of Head Start Research Since 1969." Paper presented at the 1977 Annual Meeting of the American Association for the Advancement of Science, Denver.

Manpower Demonstration Research Corporation. 1980. *Summary and Findings of the National Supported Work Demonstration*. New York: Ballinger.

————. 1985. "Job Start: Report One." New York: Manpower Demonstration Research Corporation.

McGuire, C. C. 1981. *International Housing Policies: A Comparative Analysis.* Lexington, Mass.: Lexington Books.

McLanahan, S. 1985. "Family Structure and the Reproduction of Poverty." *American Journal of Sociology* 90(4): 873–901.

————. 1988. "Intergenerational Consequences of Family Disruptions." *American Journal of Sociology* 94(1) July: 130–152.

Milgram, G. 1984. "Trends in Funding and Number of Households in HUD-Assisted Housing: Fiscal Years 1974–1984." Budget of the U.S. Government, Fiscal Year 1986, Appendix. Washington, D.C.: GPO.

Miller, T. I. 1984. "The Effects of Employer Sponsored Child Care on Employee Absenteeism, Turnover, Productivity, Recruitment or Job Satisfaction: What Is Claimed and What Is Known." *Personnel Psychology* 37: 277–289.

Miller, A. C. 1975. "Health Care of Children and Youth in America." *American Journal of Public Health* 65 (April): 353–358.

Moffitt, R., and Wolf D. A. 1987. "The Effect of the 1981 Omnibus Budget Reconciliation Act on Welfare Recipients and Work Incentives." *Social Service Review* 61: 247–260.

Moles, O. C. 1979. "Public Welfare Payments and Marital Dissolution: A Review of Recent Studies." In *Divorce and Separation: Context, Causes, and Consequences.* ed. G. Levinger and O. C. Moles. New York: Basic Books.

Moore, K., and Burt, M. 1981. *Teenage Childbearing and Welfare: Policy Perspectives on Sexual Activity, Pregnancy, and Public Dependency.* Washington, D.C.: Urban Institute.

Moore, K., and Caldwell, S. 1976. *Out-of-Wedlock Pregnancy and Childbearing.* Washington, D.C.: Urban Institute.

————. 1977. "The Effect of Government Policies on Out-of-Wedlock Sex and Pregnancy." *Family Planning Perspective* 9(1) July–August: 71–93.

Moore, K., and Waite, L. 1981. "Marital Dissolution, Early Motherhood and Early Marriage." *Social Forces* 60 (September): 20–40.

Moscovice, I., and Craig, W. 1983. "The Impact of Federal Cutbacks on Working AFDC Recipients in Minnesota." University of Minnesota, Minneapolis (December).

Mulroy, E. A., ed. 1988. *Women as Single Parents: Confronting Institutional Barriers in the Courts, the Workplace, and the Housing Market.* Dover, Mass.: Auburn House.

Murphy, I. L. 1973. *Public Policy on the Status of Women.* Lexington, Mass.: Heath.

Murray, C. 1984. *Losing Ground: American Social Policy.* New York: Basic Books.

National Black Child Development Institute. 1983. *The Status of Black Children in 1980: A Response to the President's Budget for Fiscal Year 1983.* Washington, D.C.

National Center for Health Statistics. 1982. "Advance Report of Final Mortality Statistics Report." *Monthly Vital Statistics Report* 31(16) Supplement.

National Committee on Pay Equity. 1984. *Who's Working for Working Women.* Washington, D.C.: GPO.

National Forum Foundation. 1985. *Child Support Enforcement: Unequal Protection under the Law.* Washington, D.C.

Navarro, V. 1989. "Why Some Countries Have National Health Insurance, Others Have National Health Services, and the U.S. Has Neither." *Social Science and Medicine* 28: 887–898.

New York Times. 1985a. "Cost of Care of 'Latchkey Children' Debated." August 7, pp. 1, 12.

New York Times. 1985b. "More Corporations Are Offering Child Care." June 21, p. 25.

New York Times. 1985c. "Survey Reveals Lack of Health Care." October 7, p. 7.

New York Times. 1987. "Job Rights Backed by Supreme Court in Pregnancy Case." January 14, pp. 1, 14.

Oaxaca, R. 1973. "Male-Female Wage Differentials in Urban Labor Markets." *International Economic Review* 14: 693–709.

Oellerich, D., and Garfinkel I. 1983. "Distributional Impacts of Existing and Alternative Child Support Systems." *Policy Studies Journal* 12(1) September: 119–129.

OECD. 1976. *Public Expenditures on Income Maintenance Programmes.* Paris.

––––––. 1988. *Aging Populations—The Social Policy Implications.* Paris.

Office of Economic Research. 1981. *U.S. Economic Performance in a Global Perspective.* New York: New York Stock Exchange.

Pearce, D. 1978. "The Feminization of Poverty: Women, Work and Welfare." *Urban and Social Change Review* 3: 1–4.

Perlman, S. 1984. *Nobody's Baby: The Politics of Adolescent Pregnancy.* Doctoral dissertation, The Florence Heller School for Advanced Studies in Social Welfare, Brandeis University.

Perry, K. S. 1982. *Employers and Child Care; Establishing Services Through the Workplace.* Washington, D.C.: Women's Bureau, U.S. Department of Labor.

Piven, F. F., and Cloward, R. A. 1971. *Regulating the Poor: The Functions of Public Welfare.* New York: Vintage Books.

––––––. 1979. *Poor People's Movements: Why They Succeed, How They Fail.* New York: Random House.

Plotnick, R. D. 1989. "Welfare and Out-of-Wedlock Childbearing: Evidence from the 1980s." Discussion Paper no. 876–89. Madison, Wisc.: Institute for Research on Poverty.

Polachek, S. W. 1979. "Occupational Segregation among Women: Theory, Evidence, and a Prognosis." In *Women in the Labor Market,* ed. C. B. Lloyd. New York: Columbia University Press.

Polit, D. F., and O'Hara, J. 1989. "Support Services." In *Welfare Policies for the 1990s*, ed. P. H. Cottingham and D. T. Ellwood, 165–198. Cambridge, Mass.: Harvard University Press.

Rank, M. R. 1989. "Fertility among Women on Welfare: Incidence and Determinants." *American Sociological Review* (April): 296–304.

Reischauer, R. D. 1989. "The Welfare Reform Legislation: Directions for the Future." In *Welfare Policies for the 1990s*, ed. P. H. Cottingham and D. T. Ellwood. Cambridge, Mass.: Harvard University Press.

Remick, H., ed. 1981. *Comparable Worth and Wage Discrimination*. Philadelphia: Temple University Press.

Rivlin, A. M. 1984. "Helping the Poor." In *Economic Choices: 1984*, ed. A. M. Rivlin. Washington, D.C.: Brookings Institution.

Robins, P. 1986. "Child Support, Welfare Dependency, and Poverty." *American Economic Review* (September): 768–788.

———.1988. "Federal Support for Child Care: Current Policies and a Proposed New System." *Challenge* 11(2): 1–9.

Rodgers, H. R., Jr. 1978. "Hiding versus Ending Poverty." *Politics and Society* 8: 253–266.

———. 1979. *Poverty amid Plenty: A Political and Economic Analysis*. Reading, Mass.: Addison-Wesley.

———. 1982. *The Cost of Human Neglect: America's Welfare Failure*. Armonk, N.Y.: M.E. Sharpe.

———. 1985. "Youth and Poverty: An Empirical Test of the Impact of Family Demographics and Race." *Youth and Society* 16(4): 421–437.

———. 1987a. "Black Americans and the Feminization of Poverty: The Intervening Effects of Unemployment." *Journal of Black Studies* 17(4): 402–417.

———. 1987b. "The Feminization of Poverty: Some Preliminary Empirical Explorations." *Western Sociological Review*. 15(1): 1–32.

Roemer, M. 1977. *Comparative National Policies on Health Care*. New York: Marcel Dekker.

Rosengren, B. 1973. *Pre-School in Sweden*. Stockholm: Swedish Institute.

Ross, H. L., and Sawhill, I. 1975. *Time of Transition: The Growth of Families Headed by Women*. Washington, D.C.: Urban Institute.

Ross, S. C. 1973. *The Rights of Women*. New York: Avon Books.

Rytina, N. F. 1982. "Tenure as a Factor in the Male-Female Earnings Gap." *Monthly Labor Review* (April): 32–34.

Sampson, R. J. 1987. "Urban Black Violence: The Effects of Male Joblessness and Family Disruption." *American Journal of Sociology* 93(2) September: 348–382.

Scales, P. 1983. "Adolescent Sexuality and Education: Principles, Approaches, and Resources." In *Adolescent Sexuality in a Changing American Society*, ed. C. S. Chihman, 207–229. New York: John Wiley & Sons.

Scharf, K. R. 1979. "Teenage Pregnancy: Why the Epidemic?" *Working Papers for a New Society* 6 (March–April): 1–22.

Schweinhart, L. J., and Weikart, D. P. 1980. *Effects of Early Childhood Inter-*

vention on Teenage Youth: The Perry Preschool Project, 1962–1980. Monographs of the High/Scope Educational Research Foundation, No. 7.

Scoll, B., and Engstrom, R. 1985. "Final Report of the Hennepin County Grant Purchase of Child Day Care through a Voucher System." Minneapolis: Hennepin County Community Services Department.

Select Committee on Children, Youth, and Families. 1983a. "Children, Youth and Families: Beginning the Assessment." House of Representatives, 98th Congress, 1st Session. Washington, D.C.: GPO.

———. 1983b. "U.S. Children and Their Families: 1983: Current Conditions and Recent Trends." 98th Congress, 1st Session. Washington, D.C.: GPO.

———. 1984a. "Demographic and Social Trends: Implications for Federal Support of Dependent-Care Service for Children and the Elderly." 98th Congress, 1st Session. Washington, D.C.: GPO.

———. 1984b. "Children, Youth and Families: 1983." 98–1179, 98th Congress, 2d Session. Washington, D.C.: GPO.

———. 1984c. "Federal Programs Affecting Children." 98th Congress, 1st Session. Washington, D.C.: GPO.

———. 1984d. "Teenagers in Crisis: Issues and Programs." 98th Congress. Washington, D.C.: GPO.

———. 1985. "Opportunities for Success: Cost Effective Programs for Children." 99th Congress. Washington, D.C.: GPO.

———. 1987a. "Child Care: Key To Employment in a Changing Economy." 100th Congress. Washington, D.C.: GPO.

———. 1987b. "Federal Programs Affecting Children, 1987." 100th Congress. Washington, D.C.: GPO.

———. 1988. "American Families in Tomorrow's Economy." 100th Congress. Washington, D.C.: GPO.

Select Committee on Hunger (House). 1985. *The Effects of Hunger on Infant and Child Health in the U.S.* Washington, D.C.: GPO.

Sexton, P. 1977. *Women and Work*. Research and Development Corporation. Washington, D.C.: Department of Labor, Employment and Training Administration.

Shapiro, R. Y.; Patterson, K. D.; Russell, J.; and Young, J. T. 1987. "The Polls: Public Assistance." *Public Opinion Quarterly* 51 (Spring): 120–130.

Shram, S. F., and Turbot, J. P. 1983. "Civil Disorder and the Welfare Explosion." *American Sociological Review* 76(3) November: 426–442.

Silver, G. A. 1978. *Child Health: America's Future*. Germantown, Md.: Aspen Systems.

Simanis, J. G., and Coleman, J. R. 1980. "Health Care Expenditures in Nine Industrial Countries." *Social Security Bulletin* 43 (January): 3–8.

Smith, J. P., and Ward, M. 1989. "Women in the Labor Market and in the Family." *Journal of Economic Perspectives* 3(1) Winter: 9–23.

Smith, R. E., ed. 1979. *The Subtle Revolution: Women at Work*. Washington, D.C.: Urban Institute.

Smith-Loving, L., and Tickamyer, A. 1978. "Nonrecursive Models of Labor Force Participation, Fertility Behavior, and Sex Role Attitudes." *American Sociological Review* 43 (August): 541–556.

————. 1982. "Models of Fertility and Women's Work (Comment on Cramer, ASR, April 1980)." *American Sociological Review* 47 (August): 561–566.

Smolensky, E. 1985. "Is a Golden Age in Poverty Policy Right around the Corner?" *Focus* 8 (Spring): 9–11.

Social Security Administration. 1982. *1979 Recipient Characteristics Study, Part 2: Financial Circumstances of AFDC Families.* Washington, D.C.: GPO.

————. 1983. "Monthly Benefit Statistics." No. 11. Washington, D.C.: GPO.

————. 1985. *Social Security Bulletin* 48(7) July. Washington, D.C.: GPO.

————. 1988. *Social Security Bulletin, Annual Statistical Supplement.* Washington, D.C.: GPO.

————. 1988. *Social Security Programs throughout the World, 1987.* Washington, D.C.: U.S. Department of Health and Human Services.

Steiner, G. Y. 1976. *The Children's Cause.* Washington, D.C.: Brookings Institution.

Stone, M. 1983. "Housing and the Economic Crisis." In *America's Housing Crisis: What Is to Be Done?*, ed. C. Hartman. Boston: Routledge and Kegan Paul.

Subcommittee on Public Assistance (Senate). 1980. *Statistical Data Reflected to Public Assistance Programs.* CP96–30, 96th Congress, 2d Session. Washington, D.C.: GPO.

Sulzbach, W. 1947. *German Experience with Social Insurance.* New York: National Industrial Conference Board.

Suter, L., and Miller, H. 1973. "Income Differences between Men and Career Women." *American Journal of Sociology* 78 (January): 962–974.

Sweet, J. A. 1972. "The Living Arrangements of Separated, Widowed, and Divorced Mothers." *Demography* 9 (February): 143–157.

Thornton, C. 1989. "Costs of Welfare Programs." In *Welfare Policy for the 1990s*, ed. P. H. Cottingham and D. T. Ellwood, 247–268. Cambridge, Mass.: Harvard University Press.

Tienda, M. 1989. "Race, Ethnicity and the Portrait of Inequality: Approaching the 1990s." *Sociological Spectrum* 9: 23–52.

Townsend, P. 1979. *Poverty in the United Kingdom.* Los Angeles: University of California Press.

Trieman, D. J., and Hartmann, H. I., eds. 1981. *Women, Work, and Wages: Equal Pay for Jobs of Equal Value.* Washington, D.C.: National Academy Press.

U.S. Commission on Civil Rights. 1982. *Unemployment and Underemployment among Blacks, Hispanics, and Women.* Washington, D.C.: GPO.

————. 1983. *A Growing Crisis: Disadvantaged Women and Their Children.* No. 78. Washington, D.C.: GPO.

Vining, D. R. 1983. "Illegitimacy and Public Policy." *Population and Development Review* 9 (March): 202–211.

Vinovskis, M. A. 1981. "An 'Epidemic' of Adolescent Pregnancy? Some Historical Considerations." *Journal of Family History* 6(2) Summer: 59–73.

Wagner, L. M., and Wagner, M. 1976. *The Danish National Child Care System.* Boulder, Colo.: Westview.

Walker, G. 1989. "Comment by Gary Walker." In *Welfare Policy for the 1990s,* ed. P. H. Cottingham and D. T. Ellwood, 141–145. Cambridge, Mass.: Harvard University Press.

Ways and Means. *See* Committee on Ways and Means.

Weatherley, R. 1985. "Adolescent Pregnancy; Patriarchy and the Politics of Transgression." Paper presented at the Annual Meeting of the Western Political Science Association, Las Vegas.

———. 1988. "Teenage Parenthood and Poverty." In *Beyond Welfare: New Approaches to the Problem of Poverty in America,* ed. H. R. Rodgers, Jr. Armonk, N.Y.: M. E. Sharpe, Inc.

Weir, M.; Orloff, A. S.; and Skocpol, T.; eds. 1988. *The Politics of Social Policy in the United States.* Princeton, N.J.: Princeton University Press.

Weitzman, L. J. 1980. "The Economics of Divorce: Social and Economic Consequences of Property, Alimony and Child Support Awards." *UCLA Law Review* 28: 4–21.

Wellisch, C., et al. 1983. "The National Evaluation of School Nutrition Programs: Final Report." Santa Monica, Calif.: System Development Corporation 1 (April): 4–8.

Wertheimer, R. F., and Moore, K. A. 1982. "Teenage Childbearing: Public Sector Costs—Final Report." Washington, D.C.: Urban Institute.

Wilensky, H. 1975. *The Welfare State and Equality.* Berkeley: University of California Press.

Wilson, W. J. 1980. *The Declining Significance of Race,* 2d ed. Chicago: University of Chicago Press.

———. 1987. *The Truly Disadvantaged: The Inner City and Public Policy.* Chicago: University of Chicago Press.

Wiseman, M. 1988. "Workfare and Welfare Reform." In *Beyond Welfare: New Approaches to the Problem of Poverty in America,* ed. H. R. Rodgers, Jr., 14–38. Armonk, N.Y.: M. E. Sharpe, Inc.

Wolf, W., and Fligstein, N. 1979. "Sex and Authority in the Workplace: Causes of Sexual Inequality." *American Sociological Review* 44(2) April: 619–630.

Yavis, J. 1982. "The Head Start Program—History, Legislation, Issues and Funding—1964–1982." Congressional Research Service Report No. 82–93 EPW (May).

Young, K. T., and Zigler, E. 1986. "Infant and Toddler Day Care: Regulations and Policy Implications." *American Journal of Orthopsychiatry* 56: 43–55.

Young, D. R., and Nelson, R. R., eds. 1973. *Public Policy for Day Care of Young Children.* Lexington, Mass.: Lexington Books.

Zelnik, M., and Kanter, J. F. 1980. "Sexual Activity, Contraceptive Use and Pregnancy among Metropolitan-Area Teenagers." *Family Planning Perspectives* 12(5) September–October: 111–127.

Zelnik, M.; Kanter, J. F.; and Ford, K. 1981. *Sex and Pregnancy in Adolescence.* Beverly Hills, Calif.: Sage.

Index

About the Author

Harrell R. Rodgers, Jr. is Dean of the College of Social Sciences at the University of Houston. He is a policy analyst specializing in poverty and welfare policy, civil rights, and political economics.

Dean Rodgers has written scores of books and articles on policy analysis, law and social change, and American politics and has won several awards for his work on these subjects. M. E. Sharpe, Inc. also publishes his *Beyond Welfare: New Approaches to the Problem of Poverty in America* (1988) and *The Cost of Human Neglect: America's Welfare Failure* (1982).